THE KREMLIN'S AGENDA

THE KREMLIN'S AGENDA

The new Russia and its armed forces

Mark Galeotti

Published in the UK by
Jane's Information Group Limited
Sentinel House, 163 Brighton Road
Coulsdon, Surrey, CR5 2NH, UK

Published in the USA and its dependencies by
Jane's Information Group Inc
1340 Braddock Place, Suite 300, Alexandria
Virginia 22314-1651, USA

First published August 1995
ISBN 0-7106-1384-9

Edited by Robert Hall and Peter Felstead
Typeset by Peter Felstead

Printed in the UK by Hobbs the Printers Ltd

Published monthly, *Jane's Intelligence Review* is available at an
annual subscription rate of £149 at UK rates ($250 at US rates)
from Jane's Information Group, Sentinel House, 163 Brighton
Road, Coulsdon, Surrey, CR5 2NH, UK.

Editorial: tel +44 (181) 763 1030; fax +44 (181) 763 1423;
Internet: JIR@janes.co.uk
Subscriptions: tel +44 (181) 763 0413; fax +44 (181) 763 1572.
Telex 916907

US subscriptions from Jane's Information Group Inc,
1340 Braddock Place, Suite 300, Alexandria,
Virginia 22314-1651, USA.

Tel: +1(703) 683 3700 [inside USA: +1(800) 321 5358]
Fax: +1(703) 836 5328.

CONTENTS

MAPS AND FIGURES

Acknowledgements

Parts of this book are derived form articles I have written for *Jane's Intelligence Review*, and I would thus like to take this opportunity to thank its editor, Robert Hall, for all his support and encouragement over the years. While I have valued the thoughts and advice of readers of the articles and other practitioners in the chaotic arts of post-Soviet Kremlinology, as ever my main thanks must go to those who have managed to remind me to have a life in between communion with my word processor: Mickey and our hairy, four-legged family, Ben, Sam and Katie.

FOREWORD

The speed of change in the former Soviet Union and Central Europe over the last six years has not only caught us by surprise but also challenged our capacity to analyze and deal with it. Consistently overtaken by events, expert analysts and political leaders in the West, as in Russia, now face a most difficult task — that of assessing where Russia is going and how to involve her as a partner in the solution of European and global security problems.

To this end, Mark Galeotti's book makes a most timely and valuable contribution. He lays out simply and clearly the main features of Russia's national security situation as it appeared in mid-1995. Furthermore, in his description of how the current situation has come to be, he enables us to understand, as far as is possible, how it might continue to develop. For develop it will, as the author is also careful to point out, noting those areas likely to become key issues in future East-West relations.

Russian society, and its national security system, is in the very midst of a truly fundamental transition. It is very difficult for the Western observer to appreciate fully the enormous social and political upheaval taking place, and the acute sense of instability this engenders among the population. There are resentments generated in many sectors of society by the loss of superpower states, the impoverishment of a proud nation, and the painfully incomplete dismemberment of its empire, coupled with the economic difficulties faced by the mass of the population to produce a country under the most severe stress. As the author points out, in the defence field this stress is bound to increase. Russia cannot afford a traditional Soviet-style army of the size it currently declares. The implications for further drastic change are unavoidable: we are only at the beginning of a process.

To appreciate the impact of this social revolution on our Russian counterparts, we must try to see the situation from their point of view: we must put ourselves in their shoes. This is not easy because we have been brought up in different philosophies and with different value systems. Unfortunately, this leads us frequently into misunderstanding. The Westerner who wishes to sympathize and help often appears to his Russian counterpart as condescending and interfering. It has been difficult for Westerners to shake off their Cold War patterns of thinking — to appreciate, for example, that it is not in the West's interest that the Russian defence capability collapses totally.

If that were to happen, and it is by no means impossible, the social disruption it would cause could be positively catastrophic. Russia today and for the foreseeable future will be our partner. Whatever international security structure we establish, we must in some way include, not exclude, Russia if it is to be effective. It is in our interest to help Russia achieve stability and a sense of self confidence, as well as prosperity, capable of living on good terms with all its neighbours.

In this partnership, we will of course want to work with all the various elements of Russia's national security establishment, both military and political. For that, we need an understanding of the structure of the organizations and of how they function; and, as these organizations are in flux, we need to devote a lot of effort to achieving that industry. This book makes a very good contribution to that process.

Christopher Donnelly is Special Adviser on Central and East European Affairs to NATO's Secretary General. He writes here in a personal capacity, however.

1 Decline and Fall: The End of the USSR

Mikhail Sergeyevich Gorbachev came to power at a pivotal moment in Soviet and Russian history. For decades, the USSR had been a superpower thanks to the memory of victory in the Second World War and ruinous spending upon the military and foreign aid. It had been stable, again as a result of both the legacy of fear left by Stalin's dictatorship and continued subsidies on pacifying the masses. It was run by a huge and bloated bureaucracy some 25 million strong (accounting for about 21 per cent of the entire workforce). The Communist Party of the Soviet Union (CPSU), which notionally served the working class, had in fact become a ruling elite. The million or so within the *nomenklatura* (named after the series of lists of key posts which were restricted to loyal communists) represented the Soviet ruling class. They were dominated by the *apparatchiki*, the full-time Party officials and bureaucrats.

With the death of long-serving Leonid Brezhnev in 1982, the new General Secretary of the CPSU was Yuri Andropov. Formerly chairman of the KGB (*Komitet gosudarstvennoi bezopasnosti*), Andropov was one of the few members of the Soviet elite to appreciate the challenges facing the USSR. The West, as well as parts of Asia, were going through a new industrial revolution, one of computers, information flows and post-industrial manufacturing. The USSR was still stuck firmly in an age of mass heavy industry, little changed from the 1930s. Its economy had become dependent upon oil exports, although oil prices were falling. Its military security was based upon massed armour and nuclear missiles, but the US Strategic Defense Initiative ('Star Wars') and new generations of precision-guided weapons risked making these obsolescent. Ironically enough, it took a secret policeman to realize that the USSR needed change, and it was the terminally sick Andropov who groomed Gorbachev to succeed him.

Andropov died in 1984, and after the brief stewardship of the equally ill Konstantin Chernenko, Gorbachev became general secretary of the CPSU in March 1985. He was elected from within the Party's ruling cabinet (Politburo) on the most slender of margins. While he was ultimately to come to realize the extent to which the Party's interests were not those of the Soviet people or Union, he was also a genuine Marxist-Leninist in an age of cynics. He was ultimately to fail in his epic bid to modernize and reshape the USSR but, perhaps in this context, it is more amazing that he ever tried. What is more, that he managed to break with so many Russian traditions, not least the use of mass violence as a tool of governance.

THE GORBACHEV REVOLUTION

The evolution of Gorbachev's ideas and the anatomy of the Soviet collapse sets the scene for today's Russia, and can very crudely be broken into six phases:

● **'Acceleration' (*Uskorenie*), 1985-86**

Gorbachev came to power in 1985 with no clear blueprint for change, merely a general desire to modernize his country. With his mentor, Andropov, he shared a genuine belief that the Soviet system was inherently workable and legitimate. In particular, they felt that it had simply been led away from its Leninist revolutionary roots. Stalin (1929-53) had introduced a centralization and authoritarianism which, while forging a war machine able to survive and conquer in the Second World War, had become counter-productive in a new era of high technology and light industry. As for Brezhnev (1964-82), he had kept the peace within the USSR but presided over an era of unprecedented corruption, in which ordinary worker and high Party functionary alike defrauded the state. What was needed, Gorbachev believed, was not radical reform but a controlled and limited programme with three basic elements: streamlining and rejuvenating the government system; the diversion of resources to new technologies; and a campaign against corruption, alcoholism and labour indiscipline.

The result was far from successful. The budget deficit grew steadily, not least thanks to an ill-conceived anti-alcohol programme. Intended to wean Soviet workers off the bottle and thus improve their health and labour efficiency, it simply turned them to far more dangerous illegal home brews. The state lost alcohol taxes to the tune of about six per cent of its entire revenue. Gorbachev soon realized that the USSR's problems were rather more deep rooted than he had thought.

● **'Openness' (*Glasnost'*), 1986-88**

In part as a result, Gorbachev turned instead to a very limited form of democratization best typified by the campaign of *glasnost'*. While generally translated as 'openness', the word really has greater overtones of 'speaking out'. This period was marked by an increasing candour in the official media and Gorbachev's own speeches on the state of the Union. This was not yet freedom of expression, though. There was still no political democratization and most of the media was still under tight state control. Instead, it represented an attempt to use them not to spread comforting lies but to discuss the real problems of the country. The campaign was motivated by two main concerns:

■ The task of modernizing the USSR was far greater than anyone had appreciated. Gorbachev had to highlight the scale of the problem to the elite in order to convince them of the need for more radical change. Preparing the ground from a withdrawal from Afghanistan, for example, took five years. He also needed more and more accurate information about the real state of the country on which to base his plans.

■ The old Soviet ways of managing information, largely censorship and crass propaganda, were now counter-productive. The Chernobyl' nuclear disaster of April 1986 had highlighted the extent to which the state was lying to the masses. Similarly, as the war in Afghanistan rumbled on, it was increasingly hard to maintain the fiction of a limited police action as more veterans and coffins came home. He needed to regain public trust in the state if the masses were to be prepared for the inevitable human costs of modernization.

Ironically, *glasnost'* was perhaps the most successful of all Gorbachev's initiatives. By 1988, not even the most die-hard conservative Marxist-Leninist believed that there could be any return to the old system. But words and debates do not put food on the table or modernize factories. Having established that there was a genuine and serious problem, Gorbachev was hard-pressed to find any sensible answers.

● 'Restructuring' (*Perestroika*), 1988-89
The basic problem was, after all, the economy and, here, Gorbachev cannot be described as anything but a failure — not, arguably, that anyone could have had greater success. He was, after all, faced with six thorny problems, the answers to which were often unclear, politically impossible or mutually incompatible:

■ The economy was disastrously over-militarized. Perhaps 15 per cent of GNP was spent on the military and the industries which serviced and supplied it. This sector of the economy had a disproportionate share of the best designers, workers and raw materials. The conversion of defence capacity to civilian uses, unfortunately, involves substantial up-front investment, and the USSR simply did not have the money.

■ Soviet industry was characteristically wasteful and out-of-date. It was unable to keep up with the computer revolution sweeping the West. 'A marvel of Soviet technology', a Soviet political joke went, 'the largest microchip in the world'. Again, modernization, retooling and introducting new skills are expensive.

■ Soviet agriculture was dominated by inefficient and environmentally dangerous state farms. The private plots of land which represented only four per cent of the overall area under cultivation were lovingly tended. From them came 30 per cent of all vegetables produced. Harnessing that enthusiasm to the rest of agriculture proved impossible. In part, this was a problem of resources. Would-be farmers lacked the skills and equipment with which to farm independently, given that for decades they had merely been employees on huge state enterprises. It also reflects the fact that land reform would be a huge and politically explosive undertaking, raising all sorts of questions as how the land would be distributed and to whom.

■ Soviet labour productivity was low, not least the result of the lax practices of the Brezhnev years. Then, as part of the so-called 'Little Deal', workers were given a great deal of latitude so long as they stayed out of politics. It was quite usual, for example, for workers to turn up to work drunk or take hours off in the middle of a shift to queue for food. As the Soviet saying went, 'they pretend to pay us, and we pretend to work'. Without using massive political terror along Stalinist lines, though, there was not much the state could do to change this except provide incentives. This is not only expensive but is unpopular with workers quite happy with the old ways.

■ The economy was over-centralized, run by a bureaucracy with no real interest in reform. When more small businesses were legalized by the central government in 1988, the new entrepreneurs were often forced out of business by local authorities who saw them as a threat to their cosy status quo. Whatever reshuffles Gorbachev introduced at the centre, he was never able to tame or win over the bulk of the bureaucracy which was in a position to strangle reform initiatives on the ground.

■ The Soviet economy was a deeply irrational one. Industries were sited not necessarily where it made most economic sense but where they were defensible or to satisfy a local Party dignitary. Prices bore no relation to supply and demand but were set arbitrarily by the centre. Economic realities are far more powerful than state plans, though. Money had to be spent subsidising uneconomic plants and keeping many prices artificially low. Where prices were unrealistically high, then citizens turned to the black market or simply stole what they wanted.

4

Without competition, firms became lazy. Rationalization, though, would be very painful, as the prices of many food staples would rise, factories shut and wages squeezed. Only a strong, legitimate and united government could consider such 'shock therapy'.

The basic problem underlying so many of the others was the lack of resources with which to fund reform. The Soviet budget deficit grew from about three per cent of national income in 1985 to around 14 per cent in 1989. In response, the state was forced to print more money, devaluing the rouble still further. Ordinary Soviet citizens found life getting steadily harder; the elite, resenting what seemed futile reforms, dug their heels in all the more strongly.

● **'Democratization' (*Demokratizatsiya*), 1989-90**
Radicalized by failure, Gorbachev embarked upon a characteristic odyssey of political vision and tactical brinkmanship in equal parts. He began to introduce partial democratization to the country, first with local elections then with elections to a new national parliament in 1989. In 1990, he had himself elected president, with a new array of powers. In this, he was driven by three concerns:

■ He hoped that granting the Soviet people a meaningful vote would bring them enthusiastically behind his reform programme.
■ He felt he needed a lever to try to force the Party itself to reform. By creating for himself a new post and power base as national president, he could conceivably break his links with the CPSU. At the very least, he would no longer be so dependent upon it.
■ Gorbachev was, by nature, a mediator and hoped that he could play off a Party hierarchy full of conservatives and a parliament full of radicals against each other, with himself as power-broker in the middle.

With this initiative, Gorbachev both ensured his place in the history books and doomed the USSR. The Soviet people had unrealistic expectations of this new parliament. They soon felt betrayed and looked instead to new leaders, above all the rising generation of nationalists. The parliament itself soon proved unworkable, torn by internal divisions and with no clear constitutional role. As for the Party traditionalists, they felt Gorbachev had gone too far ever to be trusted.

● **The 'Winter Alliance', 1990-91**
The winter of 1990-91 was a bleak and desperate one. War was raging

between Armenia and Azerbaijan, while nationalists were becoming dominant in Georgia and the Baltic states. In the previous year alone, GNP had fallen by two per cent. Over a quarter of conscripts eligible for the draft had refused to serve. As a result, Gorbachev flirted briefly with the idea of a return to authoritarian rule. The deal offered by senior representatives of the Party and the security forces seemed seductive. The problem, they suggested, was above all that Gorbachev was trying to reform every aspect of Soviet society at the same time. They pointed to countries such as South Korea, Pinochet's Chile and China as examples where economic modernization had gone hand in hand with authoritarianism. Time enough to democratize when the economy was looking stable. Gorbachev was undoubtedly tempted. For a short while, the signs were that martial law was soon to be declared. Hard-liners were brought in to head the Interior Ministry and a new firmness was shown towards nationalists in the non-Russian republics of the USSR. Reformist Foreign Minister Eduard Shevardnadze resigned, warning of a slide towards dictatorship and, in January 1991, troops and police attacked demonstrators in the Baltic states, killing 19. By the spring, though, Gorbachev had come to see the dangers in this new alliance. Any attempt to impose martial law would not only carry with it a real danger of civil war, it would also leave him a puppet of the conservatives.

● **The New Union, 1991**
Instead, Gorbachev took another gamble. Democratization had led to the rise of new elected governments in all the constituent republics of the USSR. He opened negotiations with them, hoping to create a whole new basis for the Soviet state. No longer would it be an empire by any other name, the new Union would be a federation of nations happy to come together for their common good. Like the European Union, member states would choose which powers and responsibilities they passed to the centre and retain their national sovereignty. In August 1991, he announced his success in hammering out a new Union treaty which would be signed on the 20th of the month. This proved to be the trigger of the 'August Coup' which broke the USSR asunder *(see below)*.

Gorbachev launched a 'revolution from above' to modernize the USSR; this triggered, and was overtaken by, a 'revolution from below' with a very different agenda. *Glasnost'* soon begot a genuine media pluralism as journalists and public figures began using the press to their own ends, often at Gorbachev's expense. Newspapers such as *Sovetskaya Rossiya* soon became, in effect, the mouthpiece of the conservative opposition. Economic reform opened up opportunities for a new generation of criminals.

Democratization proved a spur to nationalism throughout the USSR. In particular, it sealed a process which had already been under way for some time, namely the rebirth of Russia and the rise of Boris Yeltsin's Russian Federal government as a rival to Gorbachev's Soviet government.

THE REBIRTH OF RUSSIA
The decay of the Soviet state triggered a renaissance in Russian nationalism as the formerly dominant ethnic group within that state had to come to terms with not only the practical consequences of decline but also a loss of their old national identity. 'Soviet citizenship' became increasingly meaningless, while *glasnost'* brought with it a reassessment of history. The Soviet people were confronted with a string of revelations, from the atrocities committed under Stalin to the truth behind the 'socialist internationalism' which led to the invasions of Hungary (1956), Czechoslovakia (1968) and Afghanistan (1979).

In part, this was a liberal identity based on opposition to the Party. Dissidents and intellectuals championed Russian nationalism as an antidote to Soviet nationalism and tried to link it with true democratization, multiparty politics and the adoption of a free market system. What made this movement more than a marginal middle-class phenomenon was the presence of popular leaders who were able to build a bridge with the masses. Chief amongst them was Boris Yeltsin, a former Party leader who Gorbachev had first promoted and then disgraced. Fuelled both by a genuine desire to champion the rights of the people and also by vengeance, he used Gorbachev's democratization campaign to set himself up as an anti-communist candidate. He spoke to the Russian people of democracy and human rights but, above all, he presented these as the way to a brighter and richer future. This was the secret of Yeltsin's outstanding success as a politician; in his words, everyone could find what they wanted to hear.

Yet Russian nationalism was by no means unique to liberals and anti-communists. The final years of the USSR also saw nationalists who had been ardent supporters of Soviet centralism turn away from the Party. They had supported the CPSU not so much out of Marxist zeal but because they saw the Soviet state as the best and strongest structure for Russian empire. To them, it reflected all that was most admirable about the 'Russian Idea': discipline, efficiency, a concentration of forces and a self-sacrificing devotion to a greater ideal. However much they may have feared or despised particular elements of *perestroika*, the unity of the Party was sacrosanct. But as reform become revolution, they first tried to undermine Gorbachev's grip on the CPSU and then began to divorce themselves from the Party altogether.

Labelled National Bolsheviks, Neo-Stalinists, sometimes even Fascists, they took the discipline and the drive of Marxism-Leninism, but then harnessed that to a mystical, militarist and nationalist idea of Russian imperial destiny. They believed that Russia was falling apart, prostituting itself to the dollar and the deutschmark, and that only stern and vigorous action could save a distinct national tradition from being swamped by alien Western influences. This extremist ideology arose within certain circles in Moscow: communists, demoralized by the collapse of the Party; generals, cut to the quick by the decay of their budgets and prestige; and nationalists, angry that a superpower could be dismissed as 'Upper Volta with rockets' and flouted by Latvian intellectuals and Afghan tribesmen alike.

The whole question of the 'Russian identity' thus became another political battleground. There were Westernizers eager to see the country develop along European or North American lines and those who instead saw Russian nationalism being about preserving something distinctively Russian. Either way, two points were of great importance. First of all, by mid- to late 1990, both extremes of the political spectrum agreed on one thing: that there seemed no chance of the USSR surviving in its existing form. Rather, the real battle was to define what sort of Russia would succeed it. The liberals also espoused freedom for the other republics, while the conservatives wanted to preserve a Muscovite empire. The liberals idealized the West, the conservatives feared and despised it. Secondly, Boris Yeltsin increasingly stood apart from this debate. While he had risen as a champion of the liberals, he was also recognizably a patriot and much of his rhetoric could also appeal to the more isolationist and conservative nationalists. As will be discussed in the next chapter, this ambivalence about Russia's future has been at the heart of his political evolution.

THE AUGUST COUP

The coup in August 1991 was less about preserving the USSR and more about resolving this question as to how Russia would develop in the future. In this respect, easy references to conservatives and liberals mean very little. After all, the coup represented a triumph for the modern media's ability to transmit pictures, news and analysis in real-time. This triumph had a down-side, though. For the obverse was the way in which events so quickly became mythologized, crystallized in a series of striking images, convenient sound bites and comforting conventional wisdoms. In particular, two myths about the coup need dissecting:

■ **Heirs of Stalin**. The first myth is that the junta had some plan to 'put the clock back' to a Marxist-Leninist golden age. Its aims and pronouncements were actually strikingly bare of communist rhetoric.

While all the *Vosmyorka* (Octet) of its leaders were members, the Party played no real role in their plans. Instead, the coup was based firmly in three specific and overlapping groupings within the central leadership: the state bureaucrats, the military-industrial commission (VPK — *Voenno-promyshlennaya komissiya*), and the security forces. National leader and USSR Vice-President Gennadi Yanaev and USSR Prime Minister Valentin Pavlov represented the *apparatchiki*, closely affiliated with their counterparts in the VPK, namely Oleg Baklanov, Aleksandr Tizyakov and Vasilii Starodubtsev. Like the security troika of Defence Minister Yazov, KGB chief Kryuchkov and Interior Minister Pugo, they all felt marginalized and threatened by the pace of reform. The junta's appeal to the country, though, was devoid of ideology, even opening with the word 'compatriots' rather than 'comrades'. In its warning that 'a mortal danger looms large over our great Motherland', it was eerily reminiscent of nothing so much as Stalin's appeal to the nation of July 1941, ideology jettisoned in an instant to tap instead deeper traditions and patriotism.

■ **People power**. The second myth is that of people power, that the coup's failure was down to a mobilized public consensus able to bring tanks grinding to a stop. Part and parcel is the Yeltsin myth that makes his stand atop a personnel carrier in Moscow the focus uniting the collective farmer in Tashkent and the interior decorator in Vilnius in opposition to the junta. This is not in any way to denigrate the bravery of those who defended the Russian parliament building, or took part in many acts of individual and collective defiance but, rather, to state bare fact. The coup failed because of the failure of the security apparatus to support it. History is full of examples — most recently, Tiananmen Square — of civic resistance fading fast in the face of resolute and brutal coercion. The mob succeeds when it is pitted against a force unwilling to resist or demoralized to the point that it is convinced it will fail. This was as true in the victory of the Bolsheviks in 1917 as in the defeat of their successors in 1991.

There are those who see Gorbachev's hand behind the coup. They suggest that he stage-managed it from a safe distance, ready either to disavow his puppets if they failed or swing his support behind them if it looked as though the coup would succeed. There are certainly grounds for suspicion. All the plotters had been promoted by Gorbachev, and Prime Minister Pavlov had even tried to usurp some of the president's powers in June and yet remained in office.

The truth may never be known but, on balance, it is probably more the case that Gorbachev was both arrogant and trapped by an unenviable dilemma. His life had been within the Party. Still believing in Marxism-Leninism, the prospect of going down in history as the man who finally broke its grip on the USSR did not appeal. Besides, it seemed to provide one of his few credible and disciplined tools for change. Even when, by 1991, he had come to realize that it could not be a tool of reform, he did not dare

Figure 1.1: A chronology of the 1991 August Coup

The Crescendo

3 December 1990	Boris Pugo appointed interior minister; the choice of a hardline KGB veteran is seen as a portent of Gorbachev's new conservatism.
20 December	Eduard Shevardnadze resigns as foreign minister, warning that 'dictatorship is coming'.
28 March 1991	Major street protests in Moscow supporting Boris Yeltsin convince Gorbachev to move away from his 'winter alliance'.
17 June	Prime Minister Pavlov launches unsuccessful attempt to persuade parliament to transfer powers to him from the president.
23 July	Conservative newspaper *Sovetskaya Rossiya* publishes 'A Word to the People', an open letter calling for martial law.
2 August	Gorbachev announces that Russia, Kazakhstan and Uzbekistan will sign a new Union treaty on 20 August.

The Coup

19 August	At 6 am, Moscow Radio announces that Gorbachev is unable to carry out his duties for reasons of 'ill health', and that Vice-President Yanayev was thus assuming power, forming an eight-man 'State Committee for the State of Emergency in the USSR' (GKChP). The GKChP suspends the signing of the new Union treaty and declares effective martial law. Armoured columns begin moving into Moscow, while Boris Yeltsin and the speaker of the Russian parliament denounce the state of emergency as a 'right-wing, reactionary, unconstitutional coup'. That afternoon, the GKChP gives a nervous and unimpressive televised press conference.
20 August	Boris Yeltsin announces that he is assuming control of all troops on Russian soil and large crowds gather in defiance of martial law outside the Russian parliament building (the White House). After a day of stand-off, that night tanks and troops clash with defenders of the White House, killing three, but make no serious assault.

release his grip upon it. Gorbachev thought figures like Pavlov and Kryuchkov could be best controlled when within rather than outside his administration.

As it was, the abortive coup proved a catalyst: perhaps, it is better to say that it instead laid bare changes which had been taking place in the country and forced people to take full account of them. It highlighted the collapse of

21 August	The Russian parliament holds an emergency session declaring the actions of the GKChP illegal. Several GKChP members flee Moscow by air to seek Gorbachev's forgiveness, followed by a Russian team led by Vice-President Rutskoi which also leaves for the Crimea to bring Gorbachev back to Moscow.
22 August	Mikhail Gorbachev returns to Moscow; the members of the GKChP are arrested (Boris Pugo commits suicide).
	The Consequences
23 August	Gorbachev addresses an extraordinary session of the Russian parliament. He is humiliated by Yeltsin who suspends the Communist Party and warns that the new Union treaty can no longer be signed in its present form.
24 August	Gorbachev resigns from his post as general secretary of the CPSU. Ukraine declares independence from the USSR.
25 August	Belorussia declares itself independent (renamed Belarus).
27 August	Moldova declares independence.
30 August	Azerbaijan declares independence.
5 September	Uzbekistan declares independence.
6 September	The independence of the Baltic states (Latvia, Lithuania, Estonia) is recognized by Moscow.
9 September	Tajikistan declares independence.
21 September	Armenia declares independence.
27 October	Turkmenistan declares independence.
8 December	Presidents of Russia, Ukraine and Belarus meet in Brest and announce the formation of the Commonwealth of Independent States.
16 December	Kazakhstan declares independence.
25 December	Gorbachev resigns as Soviet president.
31 December	USSR formally dissolved.

the unity of the Soviet elite, above all of the security forces. That the police *(militsiya)* were prepared to ignore the centre was perhaps least surprising. Since mid-1990, the trend had been for devolution, first with the 'Tol'yatti model' which was an experimental police reform whereby industrial enterprises sponsored local police, then the 'Municipal Militia' scheme which established forces paid for by local authorities. Locally recruited and housed, the police proved unprepared to adopt a political role. The Interior Ministry's Interior Troops and Special Designation Police Detachment (OMON — *Otryad militsii osobennovo naznacheniya*) were also divided, and scattered throughout the country. The regular army was similarly disinclined on the whole to support the junta. In Leningrad, for example, the commander of the Military District, Colonel General Samsonov, struck a deal directly with the city's elected mayor. The KGB fell apart: some 70 per cent of regional commands simply refused to follow the junta's orders. Without legitimacy, without a united elite and without a disciplined security apparatus, the USSR simply unravelled.

Gorbachev thus set out to modernize and preserve the USSR and, in the process, destroyed it. Yet, what he destroyed was its central structure. This was survived by many of the ideas, leaders and organizations which shaped it. The new generation of leaders are largely veterans of the old order. Many of these new states, for all their new-found commitment to the market, share many features with the USSR.

2 Yeltsin's Russia

While one should be cautious about pushing the analogy too far, parallels between the events of 1991 and the Bolshevik Revolution of 1917 can be striking. Following the abdication of the tsar, Russia experienced what is sometimes called a period of 'dual power' between the elected liberal gentry and bourgeois provisional government as one element and the radical Soviets (or 'councils') in the army and urban workforce as the other. This actually meant 'no power'. Each blocked the other, and thus Lenin's communists did not so much topple a government as fill a power vacuum when they launched their revolution eight months later.

Similarly, the new post-Soviet states simply filled a vacuum. Reformists and conservatives had battled with each other to a standstill, and the coup simply revealed that for all to see. What is more, the dissolution of the USSR had been taking place under the surface for a long time. During the 1970s, the elite had already begun to divide the country between them, regional Party bosses and the heads of major interest groups effectively becoming the dukes and barons of the Soviet order. The 1980s saw the process accelerate and spread. The USSR slowly atomized, with individual republics, towns, villages, farms, factories and families seeking their own answers to the common problems of shortage, hunger, disillusion and decay.

BORIS YELTSIN: FROM RADICAL TO CONSERVATIVE
Yeltsin certainly lost no time in consolidating his hold on power. The coup collapsed on 22 August and the next day he suspended the CPSU's activities throughout Russia. By the end of the year, the Party had been banned outright, Gorbachev's hopes of reconstituting the Union had been dashed and the USSR formally abolished. The Russian parliament had agreed to grant Yeltsin extraordinary powers and a new 'government of reforms' had been created with him at its head. He had certainly come a long way.

Born in 1931, Boris Yeltsin had been a career Party bureaucrat. Most of his life had been spent in the industrial city of Sverdlovsk (since renamed Yekaterinburg) in western Siberia. There he rose to become regional first secretary (Party boss) in 1976 on the strength of his reputation as a no-nonsense administrator. In 1985, he was brought to Moscow with a new job in the central Party apparatus and, six months later, Gorbachev appointed him in charge of Moscow. He badly misjudged the politics of the city, though, and his high-profile campaigns against corruption and waste soon alienated many powerful interest groups. When he spoke out against the slow pace of reform at a meeting of the Party Central Committee in October 1987, Yeltsin convinced Gorbachev that he had become a liability, not an asset. He was duly sacked in November. Yeltsin threw himself into opposition politics, taking full advantage of democratization to establish himself as a champion of the masses. In 1989, he was elected to the new parliament where he founded a democratic political grouping and, in 1990, he went on to be elected president of the Russian Federation.

In opposition, his rhetoric had been radical and democratic. At that fateful meeting of the Central Committee, he had called for a new political system, one 'which does not create leader figures and leadership, and will create popular sovereignty backed by firm guarantees of its permanence'. In office, though, the instincts of Yeltsin, the Party boss, soon began to reassert themselves. Initial radicalism soon gave way to a more flexible and pragmatic mix of short- and long-term measures. Yeltsin's commitment to democracy in principle soon began to break down when it meant legitimizing resistance to his presidential will.

Consider his economic policies. At the end of 1991, Yeltsin seemed eager to abandon the muddled half-reforms of the Gorbachev era. Under the influence of his then-confidante Gennadi Burbulis and Yegor Gaidar, a radical young economist, he opted for a course of 'shock therapy'. This reasons that a log-jammed state-controlled economy in the doldrums needs a violent jolt to force it into motion, best delivered by a dramatic liberalization removing all sorts of controls on the market. The social costs would be high in terms of rising prices, growing unemployment and falling wages but this would be a necessary price. The results were more shocking than therapeutic. In 1992, Russia's economic depression deepened to the point where in terms of output, it was worse than the Great Depression of the 1930s in the West. Wholesale prices rose by 3400 per cent and the money supply increased more than ten-fold. Exports for the first half of 1992 were 35 per cent down on the same period last year, while in the whole of 1992 GNP and industrial production both fell 19 per cent. Food production fell by 15 per cent, while the first three months of 1993 alone saw industrial production decline by almost 20 per cent.

These gloomy statistics should be taken in context, though. Russia had inherited a falling GNP (down 17 per cent in 1991), and a tax system in such disarray that balancing the budget was inconceivable. Besides, many of the problems of post-Soviet Russia's first year and a half were the painful products of economic transition rather than simple indices of decline. There was much more to be done, however: industries beyond salvage to be run down, employees taken away from production and put into training, and infrastructure brought out of service for thorough renovation. Capitalism is not such a natural state: it is not just about buying and selling, it needs a complex support environment of skills, laws, institutions and attitudes. Former Soviets were, and are, learning a new range of skills, from managing to marketing, business accountancy to insurance. They also had to take to heart the importance of the long term over the short term, of producing over trading. For too many, capitalism simply meant get-rich-quick wheeling and dealing, bazaar economics where a sharp deal today was better than nurturing a growing relationship because no one knew what would happen tomorrow.

Russia's transition to the market was so painful that, by the end of 1992, Yeltsin had been forced to ditch 'shock therapy' for a more gradual process and, in December, he sacked Gaidar and replaced him with Viktor Chernomyrdin. A former Party bureaucrat from the politically sensitive oil industry, Chernomyrdin was painted in the West as a dull grey man of the conservative wing. This proved unfair and Chernomyrdin grew into his office. First of all, whereas Gaidar was an academic economist, Chernomyrdin's career was in industrial management. While he did not stop the liberalization of the Russian economy, he presided over an attempt to make it palatable both to the Russian people and also the Russian elite. Gaidar was a better economist but Chernomyrdin is an infinitely better politician and maker of deals. Chernomyrdin had been a member of the Party the way so many others of his generation had because it was the only way to get on in the Soviet system. He proved perfectly able to operate in the new system. Indeed, he became one of the major shareholders in his old firm, Gazprom, when it was privatized. Under him, Russian economic management has been surprisingly successful and, by 1995, some experts were seeing stabilization on the horizon. Most importantly, though, it sets economic dogma aside and instead looks for politically feasible solutions which will promote stability, buy off the important interests within the country and promote Russian national interest.

The same transition from radical ideals to pragmatic realism was evident in all aspects of Yeltsin's policies. In foreign policy, judicious realpolitik soon won through. To Gorbachev, the importance of foreign policy had been its impact on politics at home. Demilitarization and arms cuts were first and foremost the means to reduce a crippling defence budget and open the way for Western trade, aid and technology. At other times, a strong line was purely intended to placate conservatives back in Moscow. Although Foreign Minister Kozyrev tried to introduce a more coherent and truly outward-looking rationale for Russian foreign policy in his early and more optimistic years, Yeltsin proved equally concerned to play to a domestic audience. The almost subservient preparedness to echo Western policies which marked 1991-92 gave way to a more assertive and nationalist tone, as the rise of the neo-fascist Vladimir Zhirinovsky and like-minded extremists sent Yeltsin hurrying to shore up his right flank.

ALL THE PRESIDENT'S MEN

One of the more distinctive features of the Yeltsin era, and something which helps explain this transition from radicalism to conservatism, has been the personalization of power and politics. Political parties tend to be nothing more than the vessels for particular politicians; they rise and fall in line with the fortunes of their leader. Boris Yeltsin, rather than building institutional structures of government, has tended to rely on his personal relationship with the Russian people and also with key allies. In many ways, this is a vicious circle: personalities count for more in the absence of stable constitutional structures and their importance also inhibits the creation of any such structures which could limit their power and freedom of manoeuvre. Broadly speaking, the president's men fall into three broad categories:

● **The personal favourites**

These politicians owe their places purely to Yeltsin's good will. Defence Minister Pavel Grachev, for example, is despised within the military but so long as he is useful to Yeltsin, he retains his post. Alexander Korzhakov, Yeltsin's chief bodyguard, is widely mistrusted but he has the president's ear (*see below*). Just as the president giveth, though, the president taketh away. Gennadi Burbulis had known Yeltsin since his Sverdlovsk days and had led Yeltsin's personal campaign staff in the Russian presidential elections in 1991. His reward was the post of state secretary and first-deputy prime minister, in effect making him second only to Yeltsin. For a while, his influence seemed without bounds. The CIS had been his idea, while it had been he who had persuaded Yeltsin of the need to adopt Gaidar's 'shock therapy'. Once this policy became a liability, though, Yeltsin showed no sentimental loyalty; Burbulis was sacked from all his posts in December 1992 and vanished from the political scene.

● **The 'Sverdlovsk mafia'**

Like most Soviet leaders, Yeltsin came to power surrounded by a close circle of friends, allies and hangers-on dating back to his early days as a regional

Party boss based in Sverdlovsk. There was Yuri Petrov, the first head of Yeltsin's Presidential Administration, who had been Party boss of the city of Sverdlovsk itself; Oleg Lobov, the head of Yeltsin's Secretariat, who had been Petrov's deputy; Viktor Ilyushin, another of this circle, who became Yeltsin's chief aide; and Sergei Shakhrai, Yeltsin's state counsellor for legal affairs. This group has far more longevity that the 'favourites' and a close internal network of friendships, loyalties and obligations.

● **The institutional kingmakers**
Viktor Chernomyrdin, prime minister since the end of 1992, is a perfect example of a politician powerful enough to be an ally rather than a client of Yeltsin's. Well connected to the new class of managers and economic powers, he can in many ways play his own game. Others lack Chernomyrdin's personal power but, nonetheless, are in the peripheries of Yeltsin's court because they represent some powerful institution, such as Viktor Mikhailov, minister of Atomic Energy (Minatom).

Of course, these are crude categories. Korzhakov has built up a powerful personal security service, in part with an eye towards freeing himself of dependence upon Yeltsin and elevating himself into the kingmakers. Foreign Minister Andrei Kozyrev, by contrast, does not really fit into any group. In many ways, the result is a court. Powerful grandees compete to win the ear and favour of the president, only too aware that their position depends either upon his whim or in building up strong, almost autonomous, institutional interests. This not only undermines efforts to create stable institutions distinct from the politics of personality, it also reflects a drift back to traditional attitudes of rule. The genuine democrats and radicals of the late Soviet era have largely fallen by the wayside. In their stead have risen men who, like Yeltsin, are products of the Party. Their instincts are those of the *nomenklatura* — to exclude outsiders, to suppress different points of view and, above all, to value the practical politics of power over the ideals of building a new and different Russia.

KORZHAKOV: YELTSIN'S STRONG RIGHT FIST
The increasingly conservative line was both promoted and reflected by Alexander Korzhakov, one of the most interesting and perhaps most shadowy of the personalities close to Yeltsin. He has been at Boris Yeltsin's side since 1985 when, as a bodyguard from the KGB's 9th Directorate, he was appointed to protect the newly promoted Party secretary for Moscow. A bond developed between the two and when Yeltsin was demoted and humiliated in late 1987, Korzhakov stayed with his new master, even offering to serve

without pay. During the August Coup in 1991, it was Korzhakov who co-ordinated Yeltsin's defence. His loyalty has accordingly been richly rewarded. Korzhakov is now one of the most powerful figures within the new Russia, with an almost unequalled level of access to the president and a growing security empire all his own.

On 22 December 1994, the Russian newspaper *Izvestiya* ran a headline 'Who Runs the Country, Yeltsin, Chernomyrdin or General Korzhakov?' Although the suggestion of former Prosecutor General Kazannik that Korzhakov 'runs the Kremlin show' needs to be taken with caution, it is clear that he has a powerful political position. The institutional basis of his power is the Presidential Security Service (SBP — *Sluzhba bezopasnosti prezidenta*) which was established in December 1993. He is far more than just a bodyguard and secret policeman, though. His authority is also rooted in his personal relationship with the president and his control over access to Yeltsin. This is Korzhakov's strength and his weakness, for he depends entirely upon the president for his position. As a tennis partner, drinking companion and associate of 10 years' standing, Korzhakov has considerable informal influence over the president, second only to Viktor Ilyushin. With Ilyushin, Korzhakov decides who has access to, and what information goes before, the president. Military intelligence's reports recommending no intervention in Chechnya were all blocked, for example, as Korzhakov was promoting action.

Korzhakov forever risks losing his control of intelligence access to the president, however, not least as he is something of an outsider to the 'Sverdlovsk mafia'. He is well aware of the power but also the fragility of his position. As a result, in 1994 he initiated an erratic and heavy-handed campaign to strengthen the president's political authority, both to protect his patron and also to affirm his loyalty and ability. To this end, Korzhakov has consistently tried to persuade Yeltsin to adopt a hard line in order to underscore his strength and belie widespread rumours about his ill-health. While this tough stance may seem to have led to disaster in Chechnya, Korzhakov has tried to present it as a success in that it has shown other potentially secessionist regions the devastating consequences of challenging Moscow. In particular, though, Korzhakov has taken up arms against possibly the most dangerous political threat to Yeltsin, namely the alliance between Yuri Luzhkov, mayor of Moscow, and the banking and media magnate Vladimir Gusinskii (*see Chapter 4*). If Yeltsin does go back on his word and stand for re-election in 1996, Korzhakov has a battery of dirty tricks up his sleeve. This was to a large extent the motive behind the creation in 1994 of sections within the SBP dedicated to monitoring rival political figures and parties. Korzhakov's favoured solution, nonetheless, is for the elections to be postponed on the grounds of national emergency, and he even wants to establish a Russian National Guard under his command to enforce it if necessary. It is difficult to establish just what Korzhakov stands for, though. At times, he sounds like one of the less sophisticated tsarist interior ministers, not least when he argues the case to include Cossack units within his new National Guard. At other times, he sounds every inch the former KGB bodyguard, suspicious of the West and a natural believer in 'the law of the fist' (*kulachnoe pravo*). His intervention over oil exports was certainly couched in nationalist and almost xenophobic terms. Loans from the World Bank for developing the oil and coal industry, for example, were characterized as 'wholly inadmissible' as they would 'increase dependence on foreign capital'. Yet, this is also the man who stood against the KGB in 1987 when he was fired for his loyalty to Yeltsin and then defied them again in August 1991.

Perhaps the answer is that there is no clear answer — Korzhakov stands for Korzhakov. An adventurer, his political and sentimental decision to hitch his career to Yeltsin's has paid off spectacularly. Having risen so far, the 44-year-old Korzhakov is unprepared to relinquish his new-found powers and position, and will, accordingly, twist and turn as the needs of the moment dictate. Ultimately, however, he is a widely distrusted creature of Yeltsin's whose power rests in his relationship with his patron and his security empire. His efforts to find other potential patrons has largely failed, not least given his poor relations with Viktor Chernomyrdin, the only senior government figure outside the 'Sverdlovsk mafia'. He is obviously prepared to use force and dirty tricks to prolong Yeltsin's tenure in the Kremlin. Yet, if the president dies or resolves to dispense with his faithful henchman, Korzhakov will be forced to decide whether he is prepared to go quietly. A man with nowhere to go but down and nothing to use except force is always a man of whom to be wary.

RUTSKOI AND KHASBULATOV: YELTSIN EMBATTLED

The power of men like Korzhakov and the security interests they represented truly came to light as a result of Yeltsin's confrontation with the Russian parliament in 1993. The collapse of the USSR had left Russia with no clear constitution or even a consensus on the rights and powers of the different components of the Russian government. In particular, a divide soon opened between President Yeltsin and the parliament, the Supreme Soviet. To Yeltsin, Russia's immediate needs were so pressing and the dangers of economic or political collapse so great that there was no alternative to a strong executive presidency. He could not afford to be trapped in endless rounds of legislative reviews and debates, especially not with a parliament which had been elected during the Soviet era and which contained a fair proportion of Party hacks and conservatives. Parliament, not surprisingly, saw things differently. Yeltsin was creating an elected dictatorship, and if democracy was to be brought to Russia then there had to be a strong parliament in place to make sure that no leader could rule unchallenged.

It has to be said that there are rights and wrongs on both sides. In the final analysis, though, the growing dispute between parliament and president through 1992 and 1993 represented a serious threat to the new Russian state. In December 1992, parliament had failed to back Gaidar as prime minister, critically undermining his standing and authority. In March 1993, there was even an attempt, albeit unsuccessful, to impeach Yeltsin. National politics were becoming dangerously polarized between Yeltsin and an ungainly opposition led by the speaker of parliament, Ruslan Khasbulatov, and the maverick vice-president, Alexander Rutskoi.

In many ways, Khasbulatov was an outstanding figure, if not always for the right reasons. A Chechen from the North Caucasus, he had, nevertheless, done well within a Russian-dominated system. He had been an ally of Yeltsin's, and Yeltsin had overridden the protests of many liberals to have him elected speaker of parliament in 1991. He soon parted company with the president, however, as he fought a running war to establish and extend parliament's say in government. There is no reason to doubt his belief that a strong parliament was a necessary part of any democracy but he also had a very clear personal agenda. He milked his office for all the perks and patronage it could provide, even establishing his own private army of some 5000 men. An abrasive individual, he progressively exasperated and exhilarated the parliamentarians, yet proved to be a very able political manager. Under him, the Supreme Soviet increasingly became a focus for open opposition to the presidency.

Yeltsin's relationship with Alexander Rutskoi had been even more complex. A high-flier in every sense, Colonel Rutskoi had been awarded the coveted Hero of the Soviet Union for his exploits as a pilot over Afghanistan. Having flirted briefly with the extreme nationalists, Rutskoi then established himself as a populist reformist within the Party, very much in the mould of the early Yeltsin. When, in May 1991, Yeltsin asked him to stand as his running mate in the Russian presidential elections, it seemed a logical and inspired choice. Rutskoi could be relied upon to appeal to the armed forces and the reformist communists. At first, this seemed a dream ticket and, during the August Coup, Rutskoi personally led the mission which freed Gorbachev and brought him back to Moscow. Close allies in opposition, Yeltsin and Rutskoi became first rivals then enemies once in power. First of all, Rutskoi resented the prominence of Yeltsin's proteges such as Gaidar and Burbulis whom he characterized as 'boys in pink trousers'. As vice-president, he expected a powerful voice in the new government: the defence, foreign policy and economic future of the nation was being decided and all Yeltsin gave him was the farming portfolio. There was also an ideological dimension to the feud. Rutskoi's nationalism was much more aggressive and populist. At a time when Yeltsin was looking to creating a new class of entrepreneurs and *biznismen*, Rutskoi began championing the masses facing poverty in the process. At a time when Yeltsin was trying to woo the West, Rutskoi denounced what he saw as the Western influences polluting traditional Russian culture. The new middle class, in his words, were rushing to 'take the sacrament at MacDonalds'.

Both Khasbulatov and Rutskoi were too powerful and outspoken to ignore or sideline easily. Khasbulatov, whatever his personal failings, did represent parliament, an institution which many — especially in Russia's regions — saw as a necessary check on the powers of the president. As for Rutskoi, like Yeltsin, he had marketed himself on who he was, rather than the platform for which he stood. Thus, he retained the potential to unite a wide range of forces, including the army and the nationalists. A war hero, with the image of a tough no-nonsense soldier, he was also popular in a way few other challengers to Yeltsin were. Yeltsin had few options but to hang on to his bitter and fractious vice-president, even though months could pass from one conversation between them to the next.

In April 1993, Yeltsin held a national referendum in an attempt to settle this constitutional stalemate. While 58.7 per cent expressed confidence in him, parliament refused to accept that this gave him a superior mandate. Besides, the support for Yeltsin was often conditional. Young entrepreneurs, for example, might support reform but not Yeltsin, while salt-of-the-earth workers could like the hard-drinking 'Boris the Bear' even while resenting the hardship and hunger his economic policies meant for them. Similarly, many of the regions which returned votes of confidence were, at the same time, agitating locally for greater autonomy. They backed Yeltsin because they thought him better for the country but were not convinced he was doing the right thing for their regions.

As a result, the very legitimacy of post-Soviet Russia was under threat. No system can survive without some form of legitimacy. This is not the same as active support. In a democracy, a citizen may despise the party in office while being a passionate partisan of the system that elevated it. Legitimacy tends to be rooted in tradition, ideology and interest, though, and Yeltsin was finding it hard to provide any of the three. His was a young state, with no real traditional roots. Nor was there any real ideology at hand to legitimize the new state — besides, the Soviet era had left the Russian people wary of anything smacking of ideology. While the system was log-jammed and corrupted, it could not bring enough of an improvement to most citizens' daily lives to win their support. This was the central dilemma for Russian democracy. Opposition, room for a plurality of opinions, and checks upon the power of the executive are vital features of a modern democracy. Yet, what if creating these also undermines the state to the point that it cannot function? Power vacuums are soon filled. Lenin understood that; so, for that matter, did Hitler, Pinochet, Mussolini and Juan Peron.

YELTSIN AND THE 'GORBACHEV SYNDROME'

By 1993, Yeltsin seemed to be suffering many of the same political problems as his predecessor. This debilitating 'Gorbachev syndrome' had four major symptoms:

■ Rapidly dwindling legitimacy, leading to a weakening of the power of the centre. Whereas Gorbachev's political skills were those of the behind-the-scenes manipulator, Yeltsin's were in the more populist arts of the democratic politician. Nevertheless, people had expected too much of him: the myth of the miracle-working 'good tsar' who could make everything turn out well was still a strong part of Russian political culture.

■ An inability to implement economic reforms which could improve the lot of the man or woman in the street. As with Gorbachev, this was both cause and effect of his personal political weakness. Also, as with Gorbachev, it reflected a central uncertainty and lack of any understanding of economics. Yeltsin's economic policies were largely dictated by a series of powerful advisers and thus changed with each new favourite.

■ In the absence of an institutional basis for his authority, a dependence on personal loyalties. Ultimately, Gorbachev and the whole USSR fell as a result of a coup launched by senior figures whom he had appointed. Some, he mistakenly believed to be reformers, others he felt were useful — as they were, in the short term — and controllable. Similarly, Yeltsin's inability to come to terms with parliament meant that he was forced instead to rely upon his 'court' and his personal relationship with the key movers and shakers of the new Russia.

■ Policies driven not by vision but by the needs of day-to-day political survival. Inevitably, Yeltsin was forced to concentrate on short-term tactics over long-term strategy.

The prognosis? Left to itself, the 'Gorbachev syndrome' was at worst a wasting disease. Yeltsin could have continued to duck and weave, deal with one immediate crisis after another, and somehow keep his country and government together until the next presidential elections. However, he did understand that this would do nothing for Russia's body politic. Khasbulatov, Zhirinovsky and Rutskoi, as well as the other contenders waiting in the wings, were thriving on the appearance of sickness at the heart of the new Russia. What is more, Yeltsin's personality was not one to flinch from stern measures. Lenin had characterized as ripe for overthrow those regimes which contract a 'critical absence of will', and Yeltsin was to prove that he still had that will. After all, he was and is a very Russian leader. At critical moments, Gorbachev had held back from using major force as a tool of everyday politics, and it was this reluctance which reflects to his everlasting credit, even if it was his undoing. Boris Yeltsin instead chose to break the constitutional stalemate by force and in doing so changed the whole basis of the new Russia.

3 After the *Shtorm*: Russian Politics and the 'Democratic Coup' of October 1993

By mid-1993, Boris Yeltsin's patience with the Supreme Soviet was exhausted and he resolved to bring a decisive end to his constitutional wrangle with parliament. On 21 September, he issued a decree dissolving it. Khasbulatov, Rutskoi and a rump of parliamentarians reacted with misplaced and violent defiance. Yeltsin genuinely did not have the constitutional right to issue such a decree and by doing so legally forfeited the presidency. Rutskoi claimed it himself but then over-played his hand by inciting armed mobs of supporters, their ranks swelled with extremists and looters, to seize central Moscow. For a moment, it looked as if they would seize the Kremlin as the city's television station fell to them. The real outcome was never in any doubt, though, as Yeltsin had already assembled the forces to win such a confrontation. The actions of the mob became the pretext for the armed suppression of parliament. On 4 August, an assault force of troops, security forces and police launched Operation *Shtorm* (Storm). Tanks shelled the White House, the seat of parliament, and commandos stormed it. What made Russia's first democratically elected leader turn on that same democratic structure? Four main reasons can be offered:

■ To break the constitutional impasse. Yeltsin saw the Supreme Soviet as a hotbed of old-style conservatives. He believed — with some justice — that it was hindering his reform plans, thanks to the lack of a clear division between the responsibilities of the legislature and the executive.
■ To eliminate personal political challenges to Yeltsin. He also — again, with reason — saw Khasbulatov and Rutskoi as threats to his personal position.
■ Courtiers and interest groups hoped to use the opportunity to their own advantage. There were many within Yeltsin's circle eager to urge a strong hand, including his close ally Gennadi Burbulis and General Kobets, his most senior uniformed adviser.
■ Parliament overstepped the bounds of political opposition. While its recourse to mob rule rationalized Yeltsin's decree dissolving parliament, it had already been acting in a way hardly calculated to win respect.

Khasbulatov had misused the patronage at his disposal shamelessly to reward supporters and buy allies, and had even established a motley personal guard of hired guns. Parliament had also shown itself unable or unwilling to accept the notion of 'loyal opposition', that is, to distinguish between issues of party or personal politics and the wider needs of the country. This is hardly surprising as it is part and parcel of a culture of democratic politics which needs time to develop but it did make it easier for Yeltsin to demonize parliament.

YELTSIN'S NEW PRAETORIANS

While the timing of the assault on the White House on Monday 4 October was precipitated by the explosion of violence on the preceding Sunday, Boris Yeltsin had been preparing for a potential confrontation with parliament since 1992. In the spring of 1993, he had explored the option of declaring direct presidential rule and dissolving parliament. The refusal of Security Minister Viktor Barannikov to enforce such measures led to his dismissal in July, ostensibly for the poor performance of his Border Troops in Tajikistan. Barannikov was replaced by his deputy, Nikolai Golushko, a former career KGB officer and a man less troubled by scruple. The heads of the three so-called 'power ministries' — defence, security and the interior — were thus actively or passively supportive of the establishment of an emergency regime.

When the fighting did start, though, Defence Minister Grachev's commitment to the forcible imposition of presidential power seemed rather less solid. Although himself an appointee of Yeltsin's, with little real future without his patron's backing, he was understandably uncertain about the advisability of involving the armed forces in internal politics. Since the days of the Praetorian Guards of Imperial Rome, soldiers can all too easily acquire a taste for kingmaking. Besides which, he had very real doubts about his authority over many units, and thus had to tread carefully lest he provoke an open split. Many units were — contrary to usual practice — moved into the city without ammunition and only armed at the last minute. It was, in fact, attempts by the anti-Yeltsin camp to encourage just such a split which convinced him, and many other senior military figures, that the confrontation needed to be ended swiftly — by force of arms if necessary. Even while the White House was being stormed, however, Deputy Defence Ministers Kolesnikov, Gromov and Deinekin were still talking to Vice-President Rutskoi, with Grachev's consent.

The Defence Ministry's rather lukewarm response ensured that the command structure which evolved was essentially ramshackle and focused on the Security Ministry (MB — *Ministerstvo bezopasnosti*) and Interior

Ministry (MVD — *Ministerstvo vnutrennykh del*). A combined operations staff was only established on Sunday evening, under Deputy Defence Minister Kobets. Even when army units did begin to be drawn into operations, their reluctance was clear. It was, for example, not a regular soldier but Lieutenant General Alexander Kulikov, commander of the MVD's Interior Army, who was appointed commandant of Moscow. Perhaps more significant is the fact that the prime mover on the Defence Ministry's side of the assault was not Grachev but Kobets, long-time rivals. The key elements involved were:

■ **The 'palace guards'.** Moscow Military District's two parade divisions — the 2nd 'Taman' Guards Motor Rifle Division and the 4th 'Kantemir' Guards Tank Division — provided mechanized infantry, as well as the tanks which shelled the White House into submission. Although historically loyal to whoever sits in the Kremlin, Boris Yeltsin had lavished particular attention on them. He had visited them in early September 1993, and their soldiers had been provided regular food supplies from Moscow depots. Even so, the commander of the 'Kantemir' Division refused to send even token forces into the city until a visit from Colonel General Volkogonov, another of Yeltsin's handful of uniformed allies.

■ **Light infantry.** While heavily armoured, the 'palace guards' were more used to parades than urban warfare. Two companies of specialized counter-insurgency troops were thus brought into Moscow from the 27th 'Teplyy Stan' Independent Motor Rifle Brigade. The principal army contingent, though, was drawn from Grachev's main — some would say only — political constituency, the airborne forces which he once commanded. Grachev ordered a reinforced battalion from the 119th Regiment of the 106th Guards Airborne Division's to be brought into the city. Like the 'Taman' Division, this unit was based in Naro-Fominsk and had been the recipient of a visit by Yeltsin in September. It participated in the final assault on the White House, losing four men. The main role of the paratroopers, however, was as a reserve. Grachev and Yeltsin knew that once they had launched their attack, they could not afford to let it drag on, lest the defenders gained new supporters or, more importantly, the pro-Yeltsin camp seemed weak and ineffectual. Hence, Grachev brought the 76th Pskov and 106th Tula Guards Air Assault Divisions to combat alert. Were the regular forces to refuse their orders, the Pskov Division would be air lifted to Chkalovskoye airfield outside Moscow, while the rest of the Tula contingent had been brought to forward dispersal sites near the city. Ironically enough, many of these deployments were based on plans drawn up, though never executed, by the plotters during the August Coup in 1991.

■ **Special forces.** Most dramatic would have been the role of the commandos of the 2nd Special Purpose (*Spetsnaz*) Brigade. Its 218th Special Purpose Battalion was brought into Moscow from the brigade's base at Chuchkov on 4 October, both to provide additional assault forces and also to reconnoitre the White House. Had the daytime assault failed, the rest of the brigade — 1500 men — would have been brought in by helicopter to launch an attack that night.

■ **The 'Dzerzhinsky' Division.** Along with the 'Taman' and 'Kantemir' Divisions, Yeltsin had courted the MVD's special Moscow guard force, the 1st 'Dzerzhinsky' Red Banner Special Purpose Motor Rifle Division. In March 1993, he had intervened to keep it in Moscow when elements of the division were due to be rotated to the Transcaucasus as part of a peacekeeping contingent. Yeltsin had made a point of visiting the unit at its base at Balashikha, 20 km northeast of Moscow, as recently as 16 September. Thus, the division followed its tradition of obeying orders: it had been one of the units to obey the coup leaders of 1991. Nonetheless, it seemed divided. Two under-strength mechanized infantry regiments were despatched, and the 3000-strong contingent failed to acquit themselves particularly well. Elements of one regiment were involved in the assault on parliament, albeit largely forming an outer cordon, vainly trying to keep rebels in and souvenir hunters out.

■ **Police.** The Moscow police force, on the other hand, had come under much firmer political direction since 1991 and provided a variety of forces for the pro-Yeltsin alliance. These ranged from the Patrol-Guard Service (PPS — *Patrul'no-postovaya sluzhba*) to the armed paramilitaries of the Rapid Reaction Group (GNR — *Gruppa nemedlennovo reagirovanniya*), as well as the OMON riot police.

■ **Anti-terrorist forces.** The operation to storm the parliament building was spearheaded by two anti-terrorist commando forces, namely the Alfa and *Vympel* (Banner) units. Alfa came to prominence in 1991 as a result of its failure to attack the White House during Yeltsin's resistance. This time it proved to have fewer qualms. *Vympel* was a more secretive unit which had been subordinated directly to Yeltsin earlier that year.

POLITICS AFTER THE STORM

It is tempting to say that Boris Yeltsin owes much to the *vosmyorka*, the octet of plotters whose bungled coup attempt in August 1991 brought the USSR and Gorbachev down. Like them, he was forced to act not wholly to his own timetable: in 1991, news of Gorbachev's bid to redefine the constitutional bases of the Union prompted the coup, while the mob violence which followed Yeltsin's decision to suspend parliament forced him to respond with violence of his own. Unlike them, though, Yeltsin made sure that he controlled the central apparatus of coercion — the MVD, the security police and the army. Of course, Yeltsin had one key advantage which the plotters lacked. They were seeking to overthrow the president and had to strike when and how they could. Yeltsin, on the other hand, could bide his time before precipitating the crisis, even if he had not foreseen the bloodshed and he had the three 'power ministers' on his side. In this, as in so many ways, Yeltsin either learned from the *vosmyorka*'s mistakes or at least avoided them. Unlike them, he acted quickly, ruthlessly and decisively.

Khasbulatov and Rutskoi were arrested and briefly imprisoned. The public purse was opened wide to buy off many of the other parliamentary deputies with offers of lucrative employment, pensions, flats and new cars. A new and less powerful Duma was formed to replace the Supreme Soviet. Grachev, Yerin and Golushko were all awarded medals for 'personal courage' during the coup, Kulikov was promoted to colonel general, and every single soldier and policeman involved was promised a pay bonus. Yet, what did Yeltsin, and Russia, stand to gain from the defeat of an increasingly impotent and marginalized parliament and how did his 'democratic coup' change Russia?

■ The constitutional stalemate was resolved decisively in favour of the president. The new Duma, while still not especially supportive of Yeltsin, has far weaker and more clearly defined functions. Undoubtedly, Russia is now a strongly presidential republic. This has been won at a high price, however.

■ Democratic ideals and hopes for peaceful reform were delivered a painful blow. Disillusion with democracy has grown steadily, breeding both apathy and extremism. In the elections to the new Duma held in December, a surprisingly high proportion of the vote went to openly anti-democratic parties, notably Vladimir Zhirinovsky's inaptly named 'Liberal Democrats'. By mid-1995, during the lead-up to the next parliamentary elections in December 1995, almost half of all Russians polled did not think they would even bother to vote.

■ The centre of gravity in Russian politics shifted towards the nationalist and conservative wing. Zhirinovsky's rise both reflected and strengthened a general trend away from the idealistic liberalism of 1991. On his release from prison in 1994, Khasbulatov noted sourly yet accurately that nine-tenths of what Yeltsin was saying in his speeches and enacting in his policies could as easily have been drafted by himself or his fellow 'conservatives'. When, in 1993, the Supreme Soviet criticized Western policy in the former Yugoslavia, it was denounced by Foreign Minister Kozyrev as neo-fascist and pan-Slav. By 1994, though, that same Kozyrev was warning that Russia would not countenance air strikes upon the Serbs in even sterner tones that those of the parliamentary neo-fascists.

■ The security forces became increasingly politicized and powerful. Once a leader is forced to use force of arms over force of argument, that leader is beholden. As a result of their support for Yeltsin, the MVD was promised a greater budget. The Security Ministry won itself immunity from any investigation of the extent to which it was simply a reborn KGB, while the Defence Ministry was given a political mandate to define its own role by framing a new military doctrine *(see below)*.

The old parliament had been a consistent and irritating thorn in Yeltsin's side. Its role had not, however, been exclusively negative. Its committees saw much useful debate, for example. More importantly, parliament was never that serious a rival to the presidency whom the constitution already gave sweeping powers. Instead, the policy impasse of the past year of so was as much the result of Yeltsin's own limitations, his habit of switching from one favourite to another, and his lack of a clear vision of reform. Of course, desperate times do sometimes require desperate measures. The question is simple: will it prove worth it?

On the credit side of the ledger, the way was cleared for coherent reform and an end to the debilitating struggle between parliament and president. It was also a powerful expression of Yeltsin's power and will, and he immediately followed it up with a challenge to the local governments in fractious regions to accept Moscow's authority. On the debit side, the coup dealt another blow to that already fragile new construction, namely the law-based Russian democracy. Less tangibly, but probably more significantly, Yeltsin upped the stakes dramatically. The elimination of parliament lost him his most effective scapegoat, leaving him ever more responsible for the success or failure of his own policies.

Similarly, his clear challenge to the regions had to be carried through were he not to lose all credibility. The danger is that if he cannot establish the legitimacy of the centre over the regions, then force will be the only option at his disposal. This is, after all, a traditional Russian response to the decay of the powers of the centre. The 'democratic coup' thus set the scene for a new era in the politics of the new Russia, one in which the battle between liberalizing impulses and authoritarian instincts has yet to be resolved.

MILITARY DOCTRINE AFTER THE STORM

The same dilemma is evident in the military doctrine adopted shortly after the coup and as a direct consequence of the army's support for Yeltsin. From the Soviets, the Russian military has inherited a way of thinking distinct from that usually found in the West. In particular, great importance is placed upon creating some conceptual model of when, why and how conflicts are likely to arise and what the appropriate response will be. While all nations gameplan and consider likely threats, the Russian approach is far more rigidly theoretical. This military doctrine then drives almost every aspect of defence policy, from determining the shape and deployment of forces to defining priorities in military research and development.

In 1990, Gorbachev had imposed a new military doctrine upon the army which was very much driven by reform. With all its talk of 'reasonable sufficiency' and 'defensive defence', it was not only a manifesto for further arms cuts but also turned on its head existing thinking. This relied on the use of massive surprise attacks and counter-strikes to win wars quickly or at least ensure that they were fought off Soviet soil. The doctrine had never sat well with the General Staff and had largely been ignored in practice. The establishment of a Russian army in 1992 once again raised the need for a new doctrine. The General Staff came up with its own proposal in May which was essentially a return to traditional Soviet practices. This was still a time of liberal idealism, though, and not only did parliament refuse to accept it but even President Yeltsin was often only lukewarm in his support.

It and three rival drafts circulated and evolved for the next year. Although the armed forces were clearly drifting rudderless in the absence of a formal doctrine, none of them proved able to win a sufficient political mandate. What won the day for the General Staff's blueprint was the coup and Yeltsin's desperate need for military support.

On 2 November 1993, the President's Security Council dropped its own version and approved the General Staff's draft. That day, Yeltsin signed Presidential Decree 1833 giving the new military doctrine full legal force. A model with potentially far-reaching diplomatic, military, economic and political implications was thus adopted as the military's price for Operation *Shtorm*. This hawkish document is above all worth noting for four main reasons:

■ It unequivocally places Russian interests above the CIS accords or the sovereignty of other post-Soviet states: there is little preparedness to treat Russia's neighbours as equal partners (*see Chapter 8*). By making the military also responsible for the interests abroad not just of the Russian state but also of Russian nationals, it carries the danger of involving Moscow in every local ethnic dispute from the Baltic to Kazakhstan.

■ It shifts the focus of Russian security concerns from the level of superpower confrontation to the need to avoid or win wars within post-Soviet Eurasia. In other words, the main threat to Russia is perceived not as major wars with NATO or China but in low-intensity conflicts, instability, civil war and territorial disputes closer to home. This is one area in which the 1993 version developed from the original 1992 draft.

■ Considerable emphasis is placed upon the state's obligations to the military. The government is called upon to protect the material well-being of the army but also its prestige and its public profile. The doctrine further states that a military threat could come from any direction, necessitating large and mobile forces. It reiterates the need for a full nuclear arsenal, a powerful navy, modern weapons, conscription, bases abroad, and a large defence industry. All this is by definition expensive, well beyond Russia's budget (*see Chapter 12*).

■ It sanctions the use of the military at home. In one respect, this was a retrospective bid to legitimize the (strictly speaking, illegal) use of the army against parliament. More generally, though, this section — again, absent in the 1992 document — lists a wide range of circumstances in which the army could be used on Russian territory, ranging from suppressing attempts to secede from Russia to fighting organized crime and drug trafficking.

At last, then, the Russian armed forces had their military doctrine. The problem was that, just as with the political mandate granted by Operation *Shtorm*, it was ambiguous and potentially dangerous. The generals seemed to have been granted the right to spend as they saw fit, even as Russia could no more afford their shopping lists than the USSR. The military had assumed or been given the right and duty to intervene anywhere in post-Soviet Eurasia, both within and without Russian borders, but will little real appreciation of the dangers in such imperial arrogance. The invasion of Chechnya, for example, perfectly illustrates the dangers of a blueprint for starting wars which says nothing about how to end them.

4 Lean and Hungry Men: Political Challenges at the Centre

Modern Russian politics are bewilderingly chaotic. Parties come and go on an almost daily basis. Yesterday's sworn enemies are today's political allies. To a large extent, this reflects the realities of a system lacking either established parties or political traditions. It is, after all, such institutions and customs which tend to bring stability into politics. Parties, for example, manage parliamentary politics where so much is decided by the quiet negotiations of the political managers of the main blocs rather than the sound and fury of open debate. They also help limit the freedom of manoeuvre of individual politicians and create some common set of ideals to which people can subscribe.

In their absence, however, politics are dominated by personalities and factions as well as individual and group interests. The basic elements of the new politics are five:

■ **The 'Party of Power'**. Concepts such as left wing or right, radical or conservative, matter far less than whether a politician is inside or outside the ruling constellation of individuals and interests. The Russians have come to refer to the insiders as the 'party of power'. While it is unfair to suggest that all the insiders are interested in is holding on to power and all the outsiders want to is become insiders, it is probably not too far from the truth. Foreign Minister Kozyrev, for example, has proved himself prepared to ditch almost all his earlier liberal pretensions to retain his position. An attempt in 1995 to create centre-right and centre-left parties under Prime Minister Chernomyrdin and Parliamentary Speaker Ivan Rybkin would not change this; behind the facade of two-party competition, the same elite would run both blocs. Very few Russian politicians can be defined by their ideology and, for most, the simple goal of politics is to win access to the 'party of power'. This is, after all, nothing new. For decades, very few members of the CPSU joined out of Marxist-Leninist zeal but because it was the passport to a good job or a better life. Old habits take generations to change.

■ **Personalities and factions**. With ideals taking second place to practical power politics, individuals and their personal followings become all important. Boris Yeltsin has his 'Sverdlovsk mafia', but so too do most influential politicians have their own circle of friends, allies, clients and hangers-on.

■ **The big battalions**. Another consequence of the still primitive nature of Russian politics is the power of key interest groups and lobbies. In some cases, as mentioned below, these are regional: in other cases, they reflect powerful institutions or even financial interests, such as the Union of Oil Manufacturers or the Imperial Bank.

■ **Local versus national politics**. While Moscow is still dominant, a great deal of power and authority has devolved to local and regional governments *(see Chapter 5)*. There are, therefore, leaders raging from Anatoli Sobchak, the mayor of St Petersburg to Konstantin Titov, the governor of Samara, who have great power within their own domains while lacking a national profile. Others, though, have managed to use their local power-bases to win influence on a national level. Yuri Luzhkov, the mayor of Moscow, is widely — if, perhaps, prematurely — tipped as a presidential contender. Others have sought to build themselves a role as the spokesman of the local barons against the centre. In 1995, Yuri Skokov, chairman of the Federation of Manufacturers, assembled an increasingly influential alliance of regional leaders. They want, in effect, their own *Magna Carta*: a sympathetic central government able to bring stability to the country while respecting their own rights and power. On the whole, they do not want to see the rise of stable party politics in Moscow, however. Such parties would soon, after all, seek to impose their candidates in local elections, while stability would limit the regions' freedom of manoeuvre.

■ **Corruption**. Russia is so deeply riddled with corruption, graft and organized criminality as to make Italy seem of haven of legality and Japan a model of open politics. In October 1992, President Yeltsin admitted that 'corruption has become the bane of life in Russia . . . [and] the time has come to put an end to empty talk on this topic'. This was just campaign rhetoric, though. There has been no real effort to root out the corruption which, after all, has been a staple of Russian political life for centuries.

Russia's current and future generations of leaders do not thus fit into any neat left-right or liberal-conservative spectrum. In some ways, this is encouraging for it suggests that some sort of consensus may be developing within Russia between, and far from, the banner-waving antics of the nationalists and communists on the one extreme and the libertarian excesses of the radicals on the other. It does, nonetheless, underline the essentially opportunistic and pragmatic nature of Russian politics. Continued uncertainty as to the health and political judgement of Boris Yeltsin raises speculation as to his likely successor. By mid-1995, his personal popularity ratings had slumped to around six per cent. The presidential elections due in 1996 thus may determine not just the policies of the new Russia but its whole future evolution. Yeltsin will go down in history as a transitional figure, the destroyer of the old order but not the father of a new one. It is thus worth looking at some of the major groups and individuals waiting to seize the opportunity to challenge Yeltsin and his 'party of power'. After all, this is a nation dominated by a 'shadow constitution' of corruption and clientship, and above all, a relative handful of key interest groups and individuals.

THE COMMUNISTS: THE VOICE OF THE PAST?

Ironically, the only exception to this rule would seem to be the rejuvenated Communist Party of the Russian Federation (KPRF — *Kommunisticheskaya partiya Rossiiskoi federatsii*). From the ruins of August 1991, the communists have built a new platform, projecting themselves as a party of common sense and the common man, opposed to the market excesses of the Yeltsin order. In the elections to the Duma in December 1993, the KPRF won more than 13 per cent of the overall party vote. Its leader, Gennadii Zyuganov, occupies a strange position, half-way between the old, even pre-Gorbachevian, Party and a West European-style socialist party. Tellingly, he has described the KPRF as the party of Peter the Great, Lenin and Zhukov: the first of these has become a symbol of attempts to modernize Russia; the second remains the icon of Marxism-Leninism; and the third, the USSR's most famous general of the Second World War, stands for national pride and sovereignty at a time when, according to the KPRF, Russia is being humbled and bought by Europe, Japan and the USA.

Zyuganov has carried out an extraordinary feat in reviving the Party after the blows of 1991 and maintaining its discipline and prestige. For all that, he is hardly charismatic and knows that he has little hope of winning the presidential elections. For the moment, he is looking either to find a more suitable front man (possibly Alexander Rutskoi) or, more likely, ally himself with some other bloc. Despite their seeming indifference to a pact, the rural Agrarian Party has many interests in common with the KPRF. Another possible ally would be Yuri Skokov's coalition of industrialists and regional interests. Whatever happens, while the KPRF is probably the single largest and most disciplined party on the political scene, it cannot win power alone.

ZHIRINOVSKY: THE VOICE OF THE ANGRY NATIONALISTS

Vladimir Zhirinovsky is perhaps the most extreme and certainly the most outrageous of a whole array of ultra-nationalists who have emerged following the USSR's collapse. Born in 1946, he studied international law and, being a fluent Turkish speaker, went on to be involved in military intelligence work. In 1990, he became leader of the Liberal Democrat Party, arguably one of the least appropriately titled organizations in the world. Zhirinovsky is a flamboyant neo-fascist who dreams of a greater Russian empire. He stood for the Russian presidency in 1991, coming third with eight per cent of the vote, yet capitalized dramatically on the backlash following the 'democratic coup'. In the parliamentary elections in December 1993, his Liberal Democrats won more votes than any other party or electoral coalition, almost a quarter of the total.

It is tempting to characterize Zhirinovsky as another Hitler — he has even written his own *Mein Kampf*. He has also penned a provocative book entitled *The Last Dash South* in which he advocates the forcible reimposition of Russian rule over the states of the former USSR (and eastern Poland) and the further expansion into the Middle East until Russian soldiers can 'wash their boots in the waters of the Indian Ocean' (*see Figure 4.1*). Parallels with Hitler, though, show both his strength and his weakness. People vote for Zhirinovsky less because of his actual policies and more as a protest against the existing order. There is no real suggestion that the Russian people have any appetite for a new round of colonial wars. Nevertheless, Hitler was ultimately invited into power by an elite who thought he would be useful to them and could be controlled. The Russian elite has no illusions about its ability to housetrain Zhirinovsky. Instead, it has moved to steal many of his clothes by taking a much stronger line on protecting Russian national interests and, otherwise, has simply ignored him.

In a way, it has worked. By 1995, Zhirinovsky is merely one more neo-fascist. His Liberal Democrats have been seriously undermined by disunity and their lack of a regional power-base. Other nationalists, such as Alexander Barkashov, head of the Russian National Movement and Sergei Baburin, leader of the Russian National Union, have an intellectual coherence which Zhirinovsky lacks. However, without his crowd-pulling populism, they can do little but glower from the sidelines. In another way, one could say that he has won. Zhirinovsky may never be president but Yeltsin's government is practising a certain amount of what he preaches, from neo-imperialism towards neighbouring states to the invasion of Chechnya. Zhirinovsky himself, though, remains a bizarre and unpredictable figure whom the political elite still treat with the mix of arm's-length caution and insincere friendliness which is usually reserved for large untrained dogs.

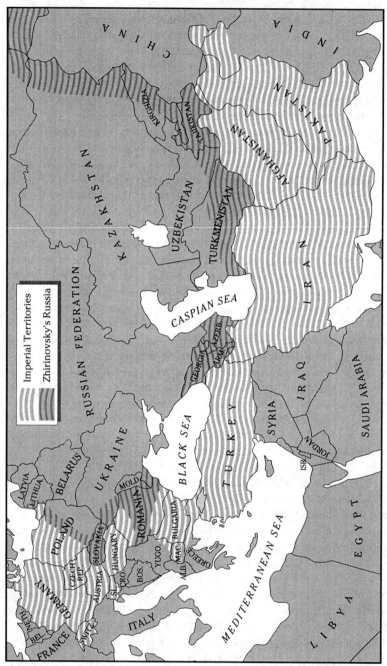

Figure 4.1: Zhirinovsky's Russia

LUZHKOV: THE VOICE OF THE MACHINE

With conviction politicians in trouble, the future looks set to belong to the machine politicians, masters of the backroom arts of patronage and coalition-building. One such is Yuri Luzhkov, mayor of Moscow. Born in 1936, Luzhkov rose through the petrochemicals industry, above all as an industrial manager rather than a Party politician. He was elected to his current post in June 1992 and since then he has made Moscow his own barony, establishing a politically powerful network of clients, allies and, some suggest, criminal partners. His power-base stretches well beyond Moscow City Council, though. He has a close political and personal alliance with Vladimir Gusinsky, one of Russia's most powerful and wealthy new capitalists. After all, Gusinsky founded his *Most* (Bridge) Financial Group on the basis of Mosstroi-1, Moscow's main construction agency.

All Luzhkov lacks is a national power-base, and Gusinsky may help provide that. The *Most* Group includes one of the country's richest private banks, a television station and a newspaper. Gusinsky's media gave Luzhkov's role in preparing Moscow for the VE Day celebrations in May 1995 especially high profile, for example. Most also has some 2500 armed security personnel, the fourth largest force in the capital. It is this powerful alliance of political and economic power which has ensured that Luzhkov and Gusinsky have become targets for Alexander Korzhakov, the head of the Presidential Security Service (SBP). Korzhakov implicated the *Most* Bank in dubious and corrupt dealing during the 'Black Tuesday' rouble scare on 11 October 1994. The most flagrant warning came in December 1994, though, when a team of masked and armed SBP officers intercepted the motorcade taking Gusinsky to work. This led to a prolonged stand-off which left six *Most* staff injured and two hospitalized. Although the Moscow Military Procurator's Office instituted criminal proceedings against the SBP for exceeding its authority, the case was soon shelved. Luzhkov is playing for high stakes and if he stands against Yeltsin or a favoured successor will have to face many more such challenges.

LEBED: THE VOICE OF RUSSIA'S SOLDIERS

Lieutenant General Alexander Ivanovich Lebed is, in many ways, the classic Russian 'fighting general': brave, outspoken, hard-bitten and charismatic. These qualities have made him a hero to many ordinary Russian soldiers and civilians and a bane of the government. Indeed, he is now being characterized by some as the next Russian president, by others as the likely founder of a martial law state along the lines of Pinochet's Chile or South Korea. However, Lebed is the archetype of the Russian officer of today, despairing of his political masters yet a fierce advocate of the discipline which, ultimately, subordinates him to them. His transition from the hero of the coup in August 1991 to the 'black general' of 1995 illustrates so many of the traits of the officer corps and highlights its mood of despair and alienation.

Lebed was born in the industrial city of Novocherkassk in 1950, 12 years before the infamous 'Novocherkassk massacre' when more than 70 workers were gunned down by security troops during a protest against a combination of food price increases and wage cuts. In the army, Lebed rose fast. Like so many high fliers of his generation, he had a 'good war' in Afghanistan, winning the order of Hero of the Soviet Union. In 1988, he was appointed to command the 106th Guards Airborne Division, becoming deputy commander-in-chief of the airborne forces in 1991. During the August Coup, Lebed was one of the few commanders openly prepared to defy the hard-liners. It was because his paratroopers were not available to provide the necessary support that the Alfa Group refused to attack Yeltsin's White House. Even then, though, it was clear that he would not fit neatly into any convenient pigeon-hole. When the radicals sought to lionize him, he tersely noted that he considered himself not a democrat but a loyal Soviet communist. He was simply unwilling to see blood on the streets of Moscow and unprepared to obey the orders of illegitimate rebels against the legal head of state.

Lebed was too wilful and outspoken for the military establishment to ignore, too popular and effective to sacrifice. The answer seemed to set him an impossible task. This was found in the secessionist 'Dniester Republic' in newly independent Moldova, mired in the civil war. He arrived in June 1992 to take charge of the Russian 14th Army; he found an army adrift. His predecessor had alienated most of his command, especially the largely locally born NCOs. Meanwhile, the escalation of the civil war caught the Russians in the middle. Lebed's response was typical: first, a decisive military response; then, political overtures from a position of strength. He mobilized the army's 59th Guards Motor Rifle Division and warned that his 10 000 troops would retaliate fully if attacked: at this time, the entire Moldovan army was only 9000 strong. Lebed then brokered negotiations. Dniester rebels, the Moldovan government, Cossack volunteers, and a whole array of different interested parties were brought together. Lebed was hardly even-handed but by the time Russian peacekeeping forces were deployed in July 1992, there was at least some peace for them to keep.

Lebed's performance sent his stock soaring ever higher. Soldiers unceremoniously ejected from garrisons in Eastern Europe and post-Soviet republics idolized him as a commander at last prepared to take a stand. Nationalists eager to rebuild a Russian empire sought to claim him as their own. Ordinary people looking for hope in a time of economic, social and political collapse saw Lebed as a new *bogatyr*, a champion. The new hero could hardly be demoted but Lebed's relations with the High Command in general and Grachev in particular continued to worsen. In July 1994, interviewed by *Izvestiya*, he even expressed his enthusiasm for General Pinochet's seizure of power in Chile. Later, he refused to allow Deputy Defence Minister Burlakov visit the 14th Army, denouncing him as a criminal who embezzled the funds of the former Soviet forces in Germany. 'Just what do you believe in?' was the furious question Lebed demanded of Alexander Yakovlev, the so-called 'godfather of *perestroika*', in 1990. It is a question which could legitimately be asked of the general, now that he has decided to engage directly in Russian politics. After all, he has been eligible for early retirement since 1994 and, with his 14th Army in the process of being disbanded, his military career was effectively over by 1995. If he is to have a public role, it is likely to be in one of three forms:

■ **'Russia's Pinochet'**. Although Lebed may have the support and the ability to launch a coup d'etat, such fears must be kept in context. His childhood was lived under the shadow of the 'Novocherkassk massacre', while it was his 106th Guards Airborne Division which was deployed in 'hot spots' from Tbilisi (April 1989) to Baku (January 1990) when other troops were being deployed to shore up the Soviet regime. Lebed acquired a strong distaste for involvement in domestic pacification which stood him in good stead during the August Coup.
■ **President**. He may stand as a contender in the 1996 presidential elections. Yet, like that other and strikingly unsuccessful officer-turned-politician, Alexander Rutskoi, he will always be a soldier at heart. Lebed has a strong sense of duty and national honour and would be a charismatic candidate. He has not the skills of the politician, courtier or economist, though. Yuri Skokov's group of regional interests is already sounding him out as a potential candidate but they see him as their figurehead, not their leader.
■ **'Voice of the Army'**. On the other hand, a recurring motif of his pronouncements is a sense of betrayal by politicians. He may thus cultivate a non-partisan role as the defender of the army and its interests and values. Convinced, as he is, that it is the armed forces which encapsulate most of what is good and worthwhile in Russian (and Soviet) life, this would give him a very wide platform on which to campaign.

A LIBERAL CHALLENGE TO YELTSIN?

As Yeltsin becomes increasingly conservative, authoritarian and erratic, it is also conceivable that he could face a challenge from liberal politicians eager to regain the ideals of 1991-92. In this context, it is alarming to see just how fragile are the positions of those politicians who could broadly be described as 'democrats'. The war in Chechnya, far from proving an issue around which moderate parliamentarians could unite against the incumbent, has instead split the camps of two of the most prominent, Grigori Yavlinsky and Boris Fyodorov. Like former acting Prime Minister Yegor Gaidar, both are economists and favour substantial economic reform, although Yavlinsky is rather more moderate than Fedorov. All three have their own parties — Yavlinsky's 'Yabloko', Fyodorov's 'Forward Russia!' and Gaidar's 'Russia's Choice' — but none has any real national constituency. A fourth outside possibility would be Sergei Shakhrai, a liberal lawyer whose 'Party of Unity and Accord' has cultivated the regional vote. He too, however, is hardly a strong contender. His woolly views have certainly failed to win the respect of hard-nosed regional politicians.

Perhaps a more serious liberal challenger would be Yuri Skokov, a man who uncomfortably straddles the liberal-authoritarian divide. He worked in the military-industrial complex and thus has a background both in real economic management and the security-related sector which the three economists lack. Having previously been close to Yeltsin, he fell foul of the president's temper when, as secretary of the Security Council, he failed to support the hardening line with parliament in 1993. He lost that job and instead began building up his own power-base. He has cleverly sought to bring together two potentially powerful interest blocs, namely the industrialists (as head of the Federation of Manufacturers) and the regional bosses. In 1995, he also founded the 'Congress of Russian Communities' whose constituency is amongst Russian expatriates and those forced to return from neighbouring nations in the aftermath of the collapse of the USSR. General Lebed addressed the Congress's inaugural sessions, and Skokov seems unsure whether he wants to move into the political ground occupied by Zhirinovsky's Liberal Democrats or assume a centrist position as a 'safe pair of hands'.

YELTSIN AND RUSSIAN DEMOCRACY

In 1995, Yeltsin came to favour as his successor Prime Minister Chernomyrdin, a man with a powerful array of allies and friends. As a result, he has founded his own centre-right electoral bloc, 'Our Home is Russia' (*Nash dom — Rossiya*). It has little real ideological basis. Instead, it stands essentially for stability and the interests of the 'party of power'. Even so, it is far from clear that it will be enough to win the day and he will probably have to forge all sorts of new alliances. This is not necessarily a bad thing. Russian politicians understand deals, as well as the making and breaking of coalitions. The very incoherence of Russian politics represents a check upon excess. Whether brought to power by a coup or through the votes of millions of disillusioned Russians, a militarist and empire-minded authoritarianism is unlikely. Too much power has passed to the provinces, local barons, entrepreneur-princes and regional commanders. The next Russian leader is likely to be a pragmatic wheeler-dealer more concerned with management, stability and survival than national glory or a new empire.

That is, of course, if it ever comes to elections. The president's closest allies — most notably, Alexander Korzhakov, but also including erstwhile liberal aide Sergei Filatov — are encouraging him to adopt one of five alternative strategies:

■ **Cancellation**. Cancelling the 1996 elections could be justified on the grounds of a 'national emergency' and delayed for either a set or an indefinite period.
■ **Gerrymandering**. Stand again on the basis of a new temporary election law strongly favouring the incumbent.
■ **Referendum**. Follow the example of the Central Asian presidents and instead call a referendum extending the president's term for another five years. Such a referendum, it is argued, would be easier to rig or manage.
■ **Declaration**. An option which would bypass the need for an election, without necessitating Boris Yeltsin's own candidacy, would be for the president to declare a successor (such as Chernomyrdin) and either impose the choice by decree or, again, subject it to a simple referendum.
■ **Cheat**. Korzhakov has an extensive 'black book' of compromising information on many candidates, the Federal Security Service has the right and ability to monitor people's ballots, the state has a wide range of powers to control the media and a deep pocket with which to buy friends and influence people. As a result, there are those within the president's circle who simply favour a crooked election.

On balance, it is hard to deny that the new 'democratic' state is dominated by an ungainly alliance of Soviet-style bureaucratic self-interest and the worst of free-market 'Wild-West economics' in which everything and everyone has a price. On one level, this need not be a bad thing. Many scholars have looked at corruption as a natural, even necessary, element of development, the process whereby a new rich class arises and a new economic system evolves. After all, endemic corruption in Italy and Japan co-existed with economic boom, while it could be argued that the periods of British imperial and US economic predominance were also marked by a rather loose adherence to the official rules of political life. Yet, corruption does pose a threat when it erodes rather than buttresses the bases of state and society. In Italy, for example, corruption worked to preserve traditions of regional loyalty and provided a keel to sail the Christian Democrat-dominated regime through the seemingly turbulent waters of Italian politics. For 40 years, the corruption of the state brought legitimacy, bought off potential threats and kept the system running. The situation in Russia is rather different.

Japan and Italy developed their complex states, rooted in a twisted tangle of corruption and legality, in very particular conditions. While devastated by the Second World War, they rebuilt under the tutelage of the USA, eager to provide the material and moral support to create states firmly within the anti-Soviet camp. Russia is engaged in a bid to redefine and recreate itself in the midst of a crisis every bit as serious. In many ways, Russia's problems are far greater. Paradoxically, building an economy anew on the burnt-out ruins of the old is easier than restructuring an existing one. Besides, without the object lesson of military defeat and Allied troops in occupation, it is harder for Russia to come to terms with the magnitude of her collapse. It is too late to wish, tongue in cheek, that the West had done Russia the favour of bombing it to rubble.

Nevertheless, through their dirty tricks, their overt use of patronage and threat, their attempts to rig the electoral system and their open disregard for the niceties of democracy, many in Yeltsin's closest circle are bringing the whole political system into greater disrepute. Even if re-elected, Yeltsin is unlikely to win anything but the most artificial of mandates and it is inconceivable that he could serve out another term as more that a figurehead. Polled in early 1995, only 12 per cent of Russians felt they could agree with the statement that 'democracy is working', and it is out of such disillusion that extremist politicians and extremist measures can emerge. Boris Yeltsin may prove to have been the destroyer not just of the USSR but also of post-Soviet democracy.

5   Holding all the Russias Together: Challenges from the Regions

Imperial Russia, one of its anthems went, was 'one and indivisible'. In fact, it was anything but. How could it be otherwise? The Russian Federation spans almost half the globe, and its population of just under 150 million comprises over a 100 different ethnic groups. Russians make up only 82 per cent of the whole, the rest ranging from Siberian tribespeople to Karelian Finns. Russia's present boundaries, after all, reflect centuries of conquest and expansion. The Federation Treaty, which was supposed to provide the legal basis for their association, was cobbled together in March 1992. Yet to sell it to the non-Russian regions, Yeltsin had to make all sorts of compromises. The result is a treaty full of holes and inconsistencies which is almost impossible to enforce. So far, only Chechnya has dared openly challenge the might of Moscow *(see Chapter 7)*. Many of the other regions and their leaderships, though, are in a state of 'cold war' with the centre, constantly trying to see how much power and revenue they can hold on to. Inevitably, this raises two associated questions: just where do Russia's natural boundaries lie; and, of greater immediate importance, just how far is Moscow able to control Russia?

Chechnya is hardly the only region in which troops have had to be deployed. Much of the rest of the Caucasus is under virtual martial law. It is not only to the south that Moscow is having trouble maintaining its authority. Organized crime everywhere has grown to the point where it undermines the legal government. Widespread tax evasion costs the government perhaps 40 per cent of its revenues and also reflects a general lack of faith in the state. The loyalty of the army itself is under question. In Siberia and the Far East, questions are already being asked as to just how far local interests coincide with Moscow's. As trade links with China, Japan and South Korea strengthen, these regions are increasingly looking south and east rather than west. Elsewhere in Russia, regions such as Tatarstan and Tyva (formerly Tuva), populated predominantly by non-Russians, are also questioning Slav control. There are, after all, four important reasons why regionalism is a serious challenge to this sprawling country:

■ **A weak 'idea' of the state**. The collapse of the Soviet Union has left Russia facing a crisis of national identity. Its borders are those of the Russian Soviet Federal Socialist Republic and its leaders largely products of that old order. Its tsarist past is a rather dubious model to which few seriously would wish to return. Is this a new Russian empire or a federation of consenting partners? While the Chechen war has answered that question rather conclusively, it is reasonable to ask whether or not the borders drawn by Stalin are suitable bounds for a democratic state.

■ **The legacy of empire**. Russia is not only a multi-ethnic empire in a post-imperial world but it also has the distinct misfortune to be a land empire. Ultimately, Britain, France and the other European colonial powers could disengage from their imperial possessions secure in the knowledge that they were safely across seas or even oceans. The Russian Federation is a patchwork of Russian, mixed and predominantly non-Russian regions, and thus the question of the relationship between these peoples is especially fraught and important. They are also complicated by the legacy of past imperial policies. Some peoples, such as the Volga Germans, went through forced resettlements or were swamped by immigrants in order to weaken them. In other regions, boundaries were drawn purely to facilitate central policies of divide and rule. The Chechen and Ingush Autonomous Regions, formed in 1922, were arbitrarily merged into one in 1934, while the Jewish Birobidzhan Autonomous Region was an entirely spurious creation.

■ **Practical politics**. The interests of the regions are not necessarily those of Moscow. Regional politicians are wary of anything which might contribute to the formation of stable political parties in Moscow, as they currently both benefit from chaos in the capital and fear that these would otherwise soon 'colonize' local politics *(see Chapter 4)*. By contrast, many favour blocs such as Chernomyrdin's 'Our Home is Russia' as they understand and can play this sort of cynical power politics. Yeltsin appointed local governors nominally to run local administrations, implicitly to build alliances between Moscow and the localities. These have proven unable to do either. Some have gone native; most who have tried to exert Moscow's writ have found themselves isolated and marginalized.

■ **Tradition**. It is also worth noting that it has always been like this. The tsars faced great problems affirming their authority across their country, while part of Stalin's savagery can be attributed to his need to cow regional interests. For reasons of geography, economics and history, this is an intrinsically unmanageable country; modern telecommunications and bureaucracy have done little to change this.

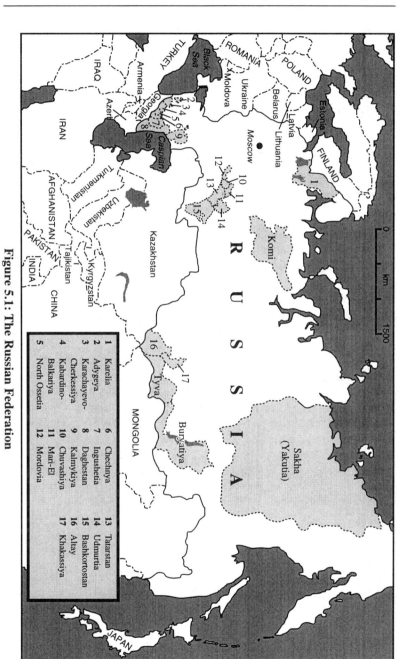

Figure 5.1: The Russian Federation

1	Karelia	6	Chechnya	13	Tatarstan
2	Adygeya	7	Ingushetia	14	Udmurtia
3	Karachayevo-	8	Daghestan	15	Bashkortostan
4	Cherkessiya	9	Kalmykiya	16	Altay
	Kabardino-	10	Chuvashiya	17	Khakassiya
5	Balkariya	11	Mari-El		
	North Ossetia	12	Mordovia		

As a result, Moscow is having to consider not just problems on her borders but the very shape of those borders and the future of Russia in her existing forms. Foreign military intervention, peacekeeping and internal security operations are all losing their distinctiveness, and the battlegrounds are creeping closer and closer to the Slav-dominated heartlands of European Russia. The collapse of the Soviet Union raised for Moscow the problem of how to develop relations with the new, post-Soviet nations of the 'Near Abroad'. Increasingly, however, Moscow is also having to consider what could be called the 'New Abroad': regions notionally within the Russian state yet in practice outside her effective authority.

Figure 5.2: The constituent regions of the Russian Federation

21 republics, 49 *oblasts* (regions), 6 *krays* (provinces), 10 autonomous *okrugs* (districts), the cities of Moscow and St Petersburg, and the Birobidzhan Jewish Autonomous *Oblast* (Region).

The Republics

Republic	Capital			
Adygeya	Maikop	0.5	22	Working
Altay	Gorno-Altaisk	2.8	31	Working
Bashkortostan	Ufa	3.9	22	Working
Buryatiya	Ulan-Ude	1	23	Working
Chechnya	Grozny	1	72	At war
Chuvashiya	Cheboksary	1.3	68	Poor
Daghestan	Makhachkala	1.8	80	Strained
Ingushetia	Nazran	0.24	71	Strained
Kabardino-Balkariya	Nal'chik	0.76	58	Good
Kalmykiya	Elista	0.32	45	Strained
Karachayevo-Cherkessiya	Cherkessk	0.4	41	Working
Karelia	Petrozavodsk	0.79	10	Strained
Khakassiya	Abakan	0.61	11	Very Poor
Komi	Syktyvkar	1.3	23	Working
Mari-El	Yoshkar-Ola	0.75	43	Working
Mordovia	Saransk	1	32	Poor
North Ossetia	Vladikavkaz	0.63	53	Strained
Tatarstan	Kazan	3.6	49	Working
Tyva (Tuva)	Kyzyl	0.31	64	Strained
Udmurtia	Izhevsk	1.6	31	Poor
Sakha (Yakutia)	Yakutsk	1.1	31	Good

THE ETHNIC CHALLENGES

The most obvious factor contributing to regional challenges to the unity of Russia is the ethnic diversity of the country. This has led to a range of historical, political and economic disputes with the centre, underlining the huge variety of cultures within this polity. The belt of ethnically distinct territories in the North Caucasus, for example, is dominated more by the local politics of clan and kin than the laws of distant Moscow. Even when and if resistance to the Russians in Chechnya is defeated, Moscow's authority will be hard to re-establish. Indeed, most of Russia's southern Caucasian states are in the midst of civil wars or otherwise largely outside Moscow's control. Since November 1992, Ingushetia has been under martial law, while Daghestan has periodically been in a state of emergency. North Ossetia has been unable to avoid involvement in South Ossetia's struggles for independence from Georgia. Refugees from the wars and feuds of the Caucasus, disputed borders, the claims of Cossack colonists and economic and ecological problems have all led to near anarchy in the region.

Another region which could become the focus of ethnic separatism is a central region around Tatarstan which also contains Chuvashiya, Udmurtia, Mari-El and Bashkortostan. In February 1994, Moscow signed a special treaty with Tatarstan which appeared to lay the foundations for a more confederal approach. On closer inspection, however, few real concessions were made. This treaty may offer a model for new accords between Russia and the regions but is hardly a great step forwards. Elsewhere, ethnic populations are largely either swamped by Slavic immigrants or largely denied any hope of self-assertion by economic or political circumstance. In Tyva (Tuva), the indigenous people have no reason to love Moscow. As Buddhist, cattle-herding Mongols, they were conquered by the Russians just before the First World War and experienced Russification, economic exploitation, Stalinist purges and even the replacement of their Turkish script with cyrillic. Its pragmatic president, Sherig-ool Oorshak, has made no secret of his emotional commitment to independence. Yet 90 per cent of Tyva's budget comes from federal funds and the country's two main industries are both on the verge of collapse. For the moment, the Tyvans — like the Volga Germans, or the Altai, or any number of other subject peoples — literally could not afford independence.

THE OTHER RUSSIAS

It is too easy to paint the regional challenge to Moscow as solely an ethnic issue, though. Perhaps the most dangerous challenges to the integrity of the Russian state come from predominantly Russian regions. After all, the non-Russian regions are to a large extent politically and economically marginal, while the Chechen war has underlined the extent to which the ethnic Russian state is prepared to use quite horrifying violence against fractious 'blacks' as Caucasians are widely and derogatively described. The Russian Federation's problems do not, however, stem purely from its imperialist past; they also reflect the degree to which this is a state unable to win the loyalty even of its Russian citizens.

There is a whole world of difference between the experiences of Moscow and St Petersburg and a handful of other centres and the cities, towns and villages where most Russians live. That 'real Russia' is a land of catastrophic environmental damage, decaying, undercapitalized heavy industry and inefficient collective farms: rustbelt, dustbelt and developing world, all rolled in to one. There are also the expatriate communities such as Kaliningrad, a fortified enclave of Russians divided from the motherland by the Baltic states. For the moment, the region has become a haven of all sorts of smuggling and shady extra-territorial financial ventures but this is hardly the basis for long-term economic or political security. If and when a choice has to be made between Europe and Russia, Kaliningrad will have to decide between ethnic loyalties and practical self-interest.

Further afield, Russia's huge Siberian territories are paradoxically both immensely rich and grindingly poor. The region contains the world's largest oil and natural gas reserves, uranium and gold, 90 per cent of the country's coal and an almost equivalent share of its timber. Much of this, though, is hard to tap, locked beneath permafrost or deep in swampy or distant forests. Standards of living in Siberia are generally low and falling. As a result, many are desperate to leave the region, while those who stay have steadily become more outspoken in their demands that Siberia should benefit from a greater share in the revenue it generates for Moscow.

Beyond that, the region is also ethnically diverse. While Russians have steadily moved or been resettled in Siberia for centuries and now represent more than 90 per cent of the total population, there are many indigenous peoples who often resent the exploitation of their homelands for Moscow's gain.

Moscow's grip upon its Far Eastern regions faces the same challenges as those which occur in Siberia but even more so. Sakha (formerly Yakutia) is the world's second largest producer of diamonds, something the local government decided to exploit. Instead of allowing Moscow to sell them and waiting for whatever share it would chose to return, Sakha unilaterally took effective control of the trade. As part of the deal, though, the republic's president, Mikhail Nikolayev, has consistently supported Yeltsin in his struggles with political rivals in Moscow. Sakha is in a peculiarly strong position but, more generally, the Far East is looking increasingly to Asia for friends and partners. Japan and South Korea are both investing in the region, while so too is China. In many ways, it is the position of Beijing which will be crucial in the years and decades to come. If China seems a stable, friendly partner, then many Far Eastern regions will inevitably come to rely on her. If Moscow becomes over-intrusive, China might even represent a more stable and powerful guarantor. On the other hand, a hostile or unstable Chinese neighbour might be the one force likely to convince the Far Easterners that they really do need Moscow.

There is also 'uniformed Russia': the army. For local commanders, desperate to hold their increasingly unruly units together, often lacking food, power or adequate housing, pragmatism is the order of the day. Abandoned by the central authorities, they look for other allies. Units are hiring out soldiers to harvest crops for a cut of the produce, repairing roads and building bridges for local authorities in return for fuel oil and heating. Some are even providing armed security guards for various private and public enterprises. Moscow does not like this but cannot do anything about it and has been forced to sanction such practice. What, after all, does the military have to trade but its manpower and its firepower? In Azerbaijan, fully operational tanks and armoured personnel carriers were sold as 'scrap' and ended up in the hands of Azeri government forces — at a price equivalent to the cost of a Lada saloon car.

People are looking to new allegiances and alliances, based less on sentiment or even affection but on meeting basic needs: food, shelter, a future, a community. At such a time of chaos and transition, it is tempting to fall back on historical analogy. When the ancient Byzantine economy collapsed, territorially based command structures looked to whoever could keep them fed and paid, and soon became the armies of local principalities. This is not a parallel to push too far but how many good Soviet officers, Russians even, have now become loyal Ukrainian, Kazakh, Moldovan officers?

CAN THE CENTRE HOLD?

The case of the Cossacks opens an interesting window onto modern Russia and helps explain some of the processes at work. Having rediscovered their old traditions over the past two years, the Cossack peoples are once again making themselves known. Cossack Hosts have been revived and have become powerful economic and political actors. Cossack volunteers have fought in Yugoslavia, Moldova, Chechnya and Transcaucasia. Cossack politicians have lobbied for a reassertion of Russian nationalism. Cossack expatriates in eastern Ukraine and northern Kazakhstan have campaigned for the reabsorption of their lands into Russia.

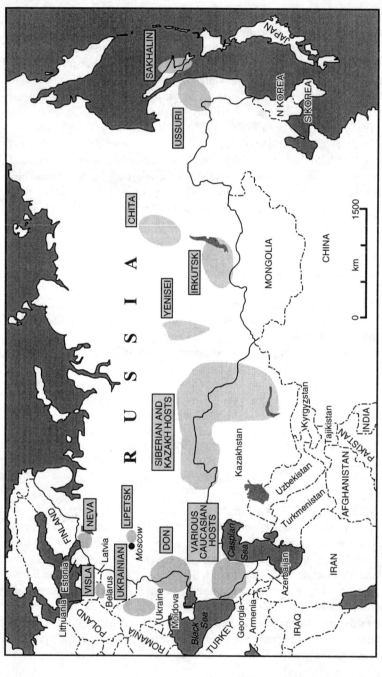

Figure 5.3: The Cossack regions

The revival of the Cossack identity is not just an interesting and picturesque anachronism, however. What the Cossacks represent is a rejection of central authority, collective security structures, multi-ethnic or - social governments, in favour of Russian unity and armed self-help; this is tribalism with Kalashnikovs. It was the process at work in the 'autonomania' of 1991 when republics sought to emancipate themselves from the Union, regions from the republics, cities and districts from the regions. It is the same process behind many of the inter-communal wars and political disputes of the region which pit Gagauz and Ossetian against Georgian, Dniester Russian against Moldovan, and ethnic Lithuanian against Lithuanian Pole. All the states of the former USSR are experiencing a crisis of authority and legitimacy. The new governments lack the levers to influence effectively their peoples and their economies. As a result, they are unable to deliver the goods, to provide the material or psychological necessities — food, electricity, transport, law and order, national pride — which their peoples are demanding. Hence people and regions increasingly fend for themselves, ignoring the centre. Consequently, the governments become even more marginal and the whole vicious cycle continues. The 'New Abroad' could quite quickly eat further and further into what Moscow regards as the heartlands of the Russian state.

6 The Hidden Threats: Terrorism, Organized Crime and the Russian State

As events in Latin America, Yugoslavia and the Lebanon have demonstrated, the dividing line between political activism, terrorism and organized crime can be hazy. What is more, such non-conventional national security threats can have an extremely corrosive effect on the state and, indeed, wider regional and global structures. The rise of terrorism and the post-Soviet mafias are thus more than a social problem, a criminological curiosity and a law-enforcer's nightmare. It also has definite implications for the national security of the post-Soviet states and, indeed, their neighbours near and far.

The problem spreads. Organized crime in Russia and the other states of the former Soviet Union is already becoming a problem for the wider world community. It is, for example, eagerly opening up new drug smuggling routes from Central Asia to Europe. The overstretched and under-supervised airports of the CIS represent an ideal transit point for couriers from Latin America and the Far East alike. As a result, street prices in Europe could fall dramatically, making drugs far more widely available. From the emigré community of New York's Brighton Beach, Russian organized crime has spread to San Francisco, Los Angeles, Chicago and Miami. Terrorism is another cross-border phenomenon; the presence of havens in Russia and the ready availability of weapons and explosives could assist a new revival of terror in Europe and beyond.

Organized crime can prevent the establishment of stable democratic states. On the one hand, criminals and terrorists can make the state look weak and irrelevant and thus not worthy of popular legitimacy. They can also undermine the stability of borders. Chinese gangs, for instance, have established a presence in the Russian Far East, especially within the large concentrations of illegal immigrants in Vladivostok, Khabarovsk and Pogranichny. Almost a third of the 17 000 Chinese citizens who crossed the border legally into the Maritime Territory in 1994 never returned. The Russian Baltic enclave of Kaliningrad is also a focus for cross-border organized crime. It has become an extra-territorial haven for criminals and shady enterprises working in the Baltic states and Poland, as well as a centre for smuggling across northern Europe. On the other hand, crime and terrorism can trigger an excessive response which may harm not only the criminals but also the very foundations of democracy. Moscow's military intervention in Chechnya, for example, may deal a blow to Chechen organized crime but it also has very serious implications for the wider Russian political scene.

NEXT STOP WARLORDISM?

A corollary of the last point is that political terror and organized crime both reflect and worsen internal political divisions. If governments seem powerless, people look to other structures which, in effect, become 'shadow governments'. This helps explain the genuine popular support some criminal groups enjoy. It also raises the danger that local leaders and even military units will increasingly carve up the country into their own little baronies. Institutionalized military criminality, after all, casts doubt upon the genuine level of control that governments and high commands have over their own troops. Many garrison commanders already see Moscow as not only distant but also increasingly irrelevant.

To expect new weak states — many with leadership structures already thoroughly compromised by association with organized crime — to face up to these threats alone is almost certainly a vain hope. Widespread corruption and organized crime and even the advent of terrorism need not mean anarchy or an end to political and economic reform. Modern Italy and Japan have both managed to reconcile the two. For a country still trying to establish its own identity from the tangled wreckage of the USSR and revive an economy moribund for decades, though, they represent a very real and serious threat.

MAFIYA: ORGANIZED CRIME IN RUSSIA

It is sad but probably fair to say that organized crime is about Russia's only growth industry. As of December 1994, there were reckoned to be 5700 major *mafiya* gangs operating in the country, controlling some 40 000 businesses, including 407 banks. Organized criminality has, after all, a long and strong tradition in Russia. Pre-revolutionary Russia was prey to the hierarchical criminal culture of the *Vorovskoi mir* ('Thieves' World'), led by the so-called 'Thieves-within-Code'. The Bolshevik Revolution did very little to change this until the 1940s and 1950s when customary barriers came down between the criminals and a new generation of unscrupulous Party bureaucrats. As early as 1956, senior 'Thieves-within-Code' met to divide the USSR between them. The 1960s and 1970s saw a steady growth in the interconnection of criminal and political circles. Russia's culture is thus fertile soil for organized crime. Russians are used to a climate of corruption and criminality in which the government is their enemy or rival. They thus

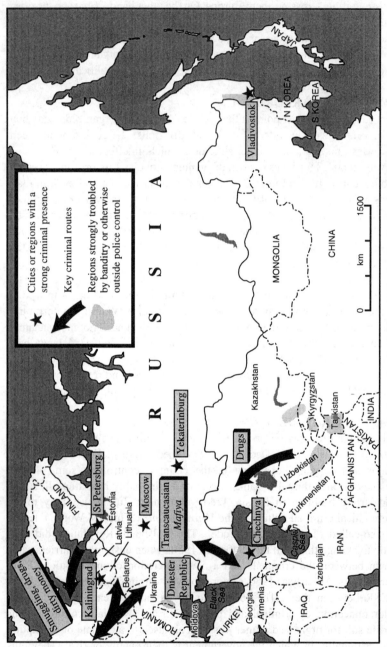

Figure 6.1: Major centres of criminal activity in the former Soviet Union

expect to have to band together in communities and alliances to fight their corner in a hostile world. The collapse of the USSR, though, has left the region especially vulnerable to a new explosion of *mafiya*. The government is largely powerless and lacking in legitimacy, creating a vacuum of power which organized crime has filled to a large extent. Economic reforms have also largely served to encourage organized crime. The privatization campaign, for example, has led to the transfer of state assets into the hands of politicians and their criminal allies and backers. Proceeds from narcotics alone were worth US$6 billion in 1994, while four out of five firms in Russia 'buy a roof' ie pay protection money worth around 20-30 per cent of their profits. Much of this has been invested through the privatization process. Viktor Ilyukhin, chairman of the Parliamentary Security Committee, reported in 1994 that organized crime controlled 55 per cent of capital in the country and 80 per cent of all voting stock, while another estimate had it controlling up to a quarter of all Russia's banks. At least 40 per cent of the money in circulation is 'dirty' and many of the major new economic players in Russia have their roots or backers in the criminal world.

While the Duma has passed several laws and motions regarding corruption and organized crime and Yeltsin has signed a number of decrees, their effectiveness has been severely limited. In part, this reflects the endemic weakness of the political system. It may also be a product of the political power and connections of the gangs. Three members of parliament who dared campaign against organized crime have been assassinated and others suspected of complicity. Central government institutions are undoubtedly riddled with corruption and thus allied with, or mortgaged to, organized crime. The armed forces, for example, have become the focus for a widespread network of mafias based in individual units and services. In October 1994, journalist Dmitri Kholodov was killed by a booby-trap with all the hallmarks of a special forces' bomb. This happened precisely while he was investigating claims that *Spetsnaz* commandos from the Moscow-based 16th Brigade were moonlighting as *mafiya* hitmen. In February 1995, General Matvei Burlakov, former commander of Soviet forces in Germany and the man widely seen as the closest to a military 'godfather', was sacked. At the same time, though, General Anatoli Salamatin, another tarnished figure, was promoted. Boris Yeltsin himself has been accused of corruption and involvement with organized crime. It has, for instance, come to light that he illegally granted fiscal privileges worth several million dollars to sports enterprises owned by Otari Kvantrishvili, a Georgian mafia leader assassinated by a rival gang in April 1994. Over 100 'Thieves-within-Code' attended his funeral.

For whatever reason, government responses have been tardy, limited and of very limited effectiveness to date. While the legal system is being revised, there is still a debilitating lag between the identification of legal needs and their provision. Nevertheless, the real problems are not in framing but enforcing the laws. While the police and security forces' budgets are receiving preferential treatment, the state is still unable to devote the resources necessary for the fight against organized crime. Under-paid, -gunned, -honoured and -motivated, the police are not up to the task. Police efforts have also been hampered by inter-service rivalries, as well as the ability of the mafias to corrupt many of the law's hard-pressed defenders.

The real problem, after all, is that Russia has for the past few years been in the throes of a root-and-branch redefinition of its identity and culture. At this formative moment, attitudes have become reinforced or entrenched thereby ensuring the continued survival and prosperity of organized crime. To many Russians, the *mafiya* economy of monopolism, racketeering and pseudo-economics is capitalism. Besides, loyalty is owed not to the state or any abstract concept of legality but to family, friends, clan, neighbours, gang or group. Even organs of government have been known to turn to the criminals for help. Many citizens and local politicians are prepared to overlook much so long as there is food in the shops and electricity in the grid. In different places, criminals have acquired roles as varied as strike-breakers, middlemen and creditors to local authorities and local law-enforcers; in turn, they are driving out smaller 'unauthorized' gangs. Further from the centre, they can also offer local advantage at Moscow's expense. In Chechnya, for example, much of the support granted organized crime was largely based on its ability to plunder Moscow and bring a proportion of the booty back home.

As a result, several criminal organizations are at work in various sectors within Russia and the rest of the former Soviet Union:

■ **Community.** In many cases, gangs are based within particular ethnic groups, such as the Chechens or the Azeris. There are other forms of community, though. Disgruntled army officers, for example, or Afghan war veterans willing to put their resources and skills to lucrative use, may bind together to form a *mafiya*.

■ **Region.** Many groups have evolved either from street gangs or, at the other end of the scale, local Party and business leaderships. As a result, their power is usually very much based on a home territory.

■ **Commodity.** Some groups are defined instead by what they do. There are specialized gangs who handle computer fraud or smuggling, for example, and have resisted the general trend towards diversification.

The criminal scene in Russia is changing, however, in a way which offers some hope. Paradoxically, it is because the powerful groups are getting more powerful and the weaker gangs are being squeezed out or taken over. This reflects the beginning of a process of consolidation. The years 1990-93 were marked by two connected struggles: first, there was the free-for-all *'mafiya wars'* between rising gangs; and, second, there was also a general battle fought between organized crime and the new concepts of legality and free-market capitalism. By 1994, the second war had been won. The gangs which had managed to establish themselves instead turned to build a new criminal status quo. Something strange is now happening. The established gangs are trying to 'launder' themselves. The proceeds of racketeering and drug dealing are being invested in 'respectable' economic power and gang enforcers are becoming 'private security guards'. The hungry gangsters of 1990 today have all the power and wealth they need and instead want the security and respect to match. They are sponsoring children's hospitals, sending their sons to British public schools and learning golf. Once they were bank robbers; now they own the banks and, suddenly, they acquire a new interest in law and order. At the same time, they are trying to keep control over a new generation of hungry outsiders. If they succeed, it is this generation of *mafiosi* and their puppets and protégés which will become the next generation of Russian political figures, big businessmen, charitable benefactors and dynastic patriarchs.

NARKOBIZNES: THE DRUGS INDUSTRY

Given the growth of organized crime, it is hardly surprising that the former Soviet Union is now the source of a massive new expansion of the global narcotics industry. Central Asia, in particular, is becoming a drugs producer to rival the traditional market leaders of Asia and Central America. In 1986, the Soviet authorities accepted that a problem was developing. Their *Mak* (Poppy) anti-narcotics operation started out as a few set-piece raids on illegal poppy, cannabis and hemp plantations in Central Asia and, within a couple of years, had become a year-round rolling programme. By 1989, paramilitary commandos were routinely involved in what were effectively search-and-destroy missions in hostile territory. Drugs, after all, were big business and Soviet power was in decline. All the post-Soviet states of Central Asia have continued their own programmes, generally still called *Mak*, even if there is a wide variation in how seriously and effectively different government have attacked the problem.

There are five main source regions in Central Asia:

■ **The Chu Valley**, stretching between Kazakhstan and Kyrgyzstan. The valley is a major source of marijuana (5000 tonnes per year).

■ **Gorny Badakhshan** in eastern Tajikistan. This mountainous region is both a source of hemp and opium poppies and a gateway for drugs from Afghanistan. The narcotics business is funding the region's running struggle for autonomy and thus the civil war against the Russian-backed Tajik government.

■ **Leninabad District** in Tajikistan, producing hemp and opiate poppies.

■ **Surkhandarya District** in Uzbekistan. This stronghold of a coalition of powerful gangs produces large quantities of opiate poppies.

■ **The Fergana Valley** in Uzbekistan produces opiates.

The truth is that the governments in Central Asia lack the resources to control drugs-producing regions. Instead, they are effectively run by local criminal organizations and clan warlords. Despite the deployment of Tajik government forces as well as Russian troops and Border Guards, Gorny Badakhshan is no longer in Dushanbe's grip. The Chu and Fergana Valleys are also largely outside the authorities' control. Besides, the drugs cartels have the resources to influence or even control local and central governments. With victory against the narcotics business apparently impossible, and keenly aware of the profits involved, it is also possible that some Central Asian government are even colluding with the cartels, seeing in them 'entrepreneurs' able to bring much-needed resources into the region at the expense of the Russians and Europeans. In 1993, for example, the Kyrgyz government contemplated legalizing opium poppy production until forced to retreat under international pressure.

Narkobiznes is not solely a Central Asian problem, though. Russia is the source of a new wave of synthetically manufactured 'designer drugs' already beginning to make its presence felt in Europe. The economic crisis has left many research chemists and pharmacists open to the lure of drugs money, as well as putting high-quality facilities on the market at low prices. St Petersburg is the particular centre for such underground activity and although 70 such facilities were uncovered in 1992 and more each year thereafter, the number in operation rises steadily. Specifically designed for maximum addictiveness and concealment, these drugs could represent a global threat to parallel or eclipse that of crack cocaine.

DEATH FOR SALE: THE RUSSIAN NUCLEAR MARKET?

Of course, the nightmare scenario has been built around the trade not of drugs but nuclear weapons. Regular accounts of alleged attempts to smuggle nuclear materials out of the former Soviet Union and the undeniable rise of organized crime have raised the spectre of an underground trade which could put warheads in the hands of criminals, terrorists and rogue states. At face

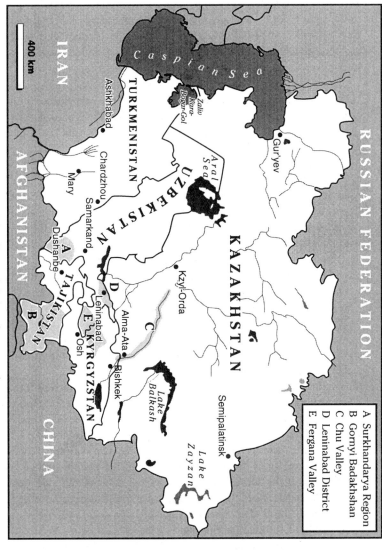

Figure 6.2: The Central Asian drugs regions

A Surkhandarya Region
B Gormyi Badakhshan
C Chu Valley
D Leninabad District
E Fergana Valley

value, after all, Russia would seem to offer everything an atomic extortionist or thermonuclear terrorist could want:

■ **Fissile materials.** There is no lack of appropriate material available to the right bidder. This is particularly true of Russia, although there is also a former nuclear warhead plant and a plutonium and uranium enrichment centre in Kazakhstan (at Kurchatov and Krasnoyarsk-45, respectively), as well as other sites in Uzbekistan, Tajikistan and Ukraine. Soviet uranium stockpiles were distributed widely, largely between Russia, Kazakhstan and Tajikistan (30 per cent apiece) with the remaining 10 per cent to Ukraine. There are also 37 civil nuclear power reactors in Russia, 14 in Ukraine, two in Lithuania and two in Armenia. Most of these run almost without outside supervision. The Russian Ministry for Atomic Energy has a central national staff of only 900. The atomic energy inspectorate, *Gosatomnadzor*, is toothless and has been able to check no more than one-third of the 14 500 organizations licensed to work with radioactive materials. Outside even *Gosatomnadzor*'s remit, there are also fleets of decaying naval vessels with nuclear reactors.

■ **Expertise.** The Russian authorities made much of their ability to monitor the activities of the so-called 'golden fund', the 2000-3000 key scientists involved with nuclear weapons programmes. This is, however, something of a red herring. The science involved is relatively simple and widely known; it is the technical problems of construction which represent a problem. The 5000-8000 technicians with the relevant specific expertise, though, have largely been neglected by the authorities and are certainly less well paid and restricted.

■ **Warheads.** Why go to the trouble of building a nuclear weapon when you can buy one ready made? Moscow's sizeable stockpiles of nuclear weapons have been swollen by the transfer to Russia of warheads from other CIS nations. Throughout the entire Soviet military infrastructure, there were 27 000 warheads in 72 Army Missile-Technical Bases servicing front-line units, and 12 'Object S' central storage sites. Over a half of the former and a third of the latter were based outside Russian boundaries and their warheads have thus had to be relocated for storage or disposal. This massive transfer has led to a 60-70 per cent overloading of Russian facilities and of the systems of monitoring their transfer and status. Although the Russian Defence Ministry refutes the claims, albeit sometimes in rather ambiguous terms, there remain persistent reports suggesting that 23 warheads were lost from a depot in Komsomolsk-na-Amure in March 1992.

There have been some, largely symbolic, measures taken by the Russians. An FBI liaison office has been established in Moscow and a joint agreement signed with the West German BND. As usual, though, the main problem is that Moscow either will not or cannot take the necessary steps, whether this involves giving *Gosatomnadzor* the powers and resources it needs or stemming the rising anarchy and demoralization within the ranks. Civil nuclear power is also vital to the Russian economy and will not be limited, while the destruction of stockpiles in line with international treaties is freeing a large quantity of new material into circulation. Perhaps more serious is the unfolding story of the 'Red Mercury' scam. Individuals close to the government and with the full backing of the security services, constructed an elaborate fraud to raise vitally needed hard currency. The government has thus — in an unlikely alliance with organized crime — already sanctioned its own illegal exports of nuclear materials. This may help explain official reluctance to give the problem the attention it deserves.

But for all that, there are important reasons why this is not as great a danger as might appear. Most of the conceivable rogue states eager to manufacture their own nuclear deterrents are amenable to carrot-and-stick diplomacy. Many, indeed, already have the industrial base to construct nuclear weapons and suitable supplies of material, yet have been held back either by the technology involved or out of a concern for world opinion. Libya, Iran and Iraq all see advantages in a nuclear capability, for example, yet are also eager to regain international legitimacy and the associated aid, trade and prestige. US pressure on North Korea and, more to the point, the Israeli bombing of the Iraqi Osiraq reactor in 1981, provide useful illustrations of the dangers associated with an attempt to build a nuclear capability.

Terrorists can also be encouraged to think twice before seeking this option. The use of such weapons, or even the threat, would make any group international pariahs. It would also escalate dramatically the measures being taken against them and provide an excellent basis for an evolution in international co-operation against terrorism. What is left, then, is simple criminal activity: bombs or, more likely, quantities of poisonous isotopes being used for extortion. Here, the only answer can be resolution and good policing. Nevertheless, it is worth noting just how reluctant even the Russian *mafiya* has been to engage in this trade. Smugglers caught to date have largely been small-time entrepreneurs and very little of their supplies of radioactive materials have been anything near weapons-grade. Even the criminals are unwilling to threaten the status quo and their understanding with the government. There is scope here to set thieves to catch or deter other thieves.

TERRORISM: A NEW THREAT

The gas attack on the Tokyo underground in March 1995 and the subsequent car bombing in Oklahoma City understandably led to a resurgence of interest world-wide to the threat of terrorism. In Russia, there are particular reasons to be aware of the problem. Not only is the country criss-crossed by the class, religious and ethnic divides which often breed terrorism but also Moscow has a pedigree as the armoury and banker of terrorists across the globe. Indeed, the Aum Shinrikyo sect behind the Tokyo massacre was strongly represented in Russia, with 30 000 members and assets in excess of US$7 million.

Even before the fragmentation of the USSR, a KGB report suggested that there were 400 terrorist organizations throughout the USSR which had been responsible for some 150 explosions in the preceding year. Of course, organized crime poses a far greater and more evident threat to public order. Of the 140 explosions in Moscow in 1994, organized crime accounted for 110. Nevertheless, there is a real and growing terrorist problem, especially in Moscow and along Russia's vulnerable communications arteries. In November 1994, a man died blasting tracks on a railway bridge across the Yauza River just outside the city, while a bomb exploded in Komsomol'skaya metro station the following month. Outside Moscow, no fewer that 16 attacks have been reported on Russian railways in the first quarter of 1995, including bomb attacks, deliberate sabotage of points and the machine-gunning of train. Overall, the main terrorism threat comes from three main sources:

■ **Ethnic minority groups**. The Chechens warned that they would take the war to the Russians through terrorist activity. This has yet to become a serious problem, largely because the Chechen diaspora is largely dominated by criminal elements unprepared to jeopardize their positions and lifestyles by taking on Moscow. Nevertheless, three explosions at the beginning of the year — in Lyublino, at the Metropol Hotel, and outside some civic offices — were reportedly the work of Chechens. The Russian authorities claim that they and the other Caucasian peoples represent the main potential source of terrorism. A series of reshuffles in the Far Eastern security apparatus, though, may suggest growing concern about the region's burgeoning ethnic Chinese population.

■ **Radical political factions**. Most such groupings tend to come from the left, identifying with European groups such as the Italian *Brigate Rosse* or Germany's 'Red Army Faction', or else the populist terrorists of late tsarist Russia. The activities of groups such as the Moscow-based 'Red Brigade' or St Petersburg 'Left Wing of the Justice Party' have of late also radicalized right-wing extremists. A recent campaign by the authorities against neo-fascist groups also risks driving their hard core underground. From whichever extreme, these groups regard themselves as fighting the encroachments of Western capitalism and the ensuing impoverishment of the Russian masses — 31-42 per cent of the population now lives beneath the poverty line. Their targets tend to be the symbols and beneficiaries of the new political and economic order.

■ **Millenarian religious sects.** Aum Shinrikyo had a sizeable following in Russia, both in Moscow and the Far East, and the authorities moved quickly to defuse any danger they might pose. In April 1995, the cult was banned. They are, however, by no means the only extreme religious groups in Russia. There are millenarian Christian cults convinced Armageddon is nigh. There are also numerous Islamic factions. As Russian forces become increasingly bogged down in the Tajik civil war and even launching air strikes into Afghanistan, the Russian authorities have warned that fundamentalists may seek to use Russian Moslems as a terrorist fifth column.

The Russian authorities have made a show of their new-found preparedness to deal with the problem. The Federal Security Service (FSB — *Federal'naya sluzhba bezopasnosti*) maintains a Counter-terrorist Directorate. Existing security units have been supplemented by an FSB Special Operations Directorate and the Presidential Security Service's *Vityaz* (Knight) commandos. Following the Tokyo attack, the Russian Ministry for Civil Defence, Emergencies and Natural Disasters has even established its own rapid deployment group in case of a repetition inside Russia. Of equal importance, Russia appears aware that terrorism is often a cross-border phenomenon and infra-CIS legal agreements on extradition and the sharing of information have been supplemented by bilateral accords and practical links between agencies. The Ukrainian authorities recently arrested radical nationalists suspected of planning a terror campaign in Russia, while the Russians deported two Turkmen dissidents accused of plotting to assassinate Turkman President Niyazov in December 1994.

Nevertheless, government successes should not necessarily be taken at face value. Many agencies have sought to play up their role fighting terrorism as a way of winning greater budgets and of legitimizing structures little changed from those of the Soviet era. The FSB, in particular, is prone to play on its struggle against terrorists and *mafiosi* as a smokescreen behind which to hide its steady reacquisition of the powers and assets of the old KGB. In addition, dealing with terrorism is seen still as essentially a problem of policing. There have been some successes, albeit usually through the application of disproportionate resources and an at best cavalier attitude towards the Russian law. Nothing, though, has been done about the underlying political and economic disequilibria behind the problem. Without that sort of political will and wisdom, then the police officers and spies can only keep the problem in check.

7 Chechnya: Fire in the Caucasus

Of all the North Caucasian mountain peoples, the Chechens put up the fiercest resistance to the Russian invaders of the nineteenth century and suffered the most for their pains. Stubbornly independent, with strong loyalties to family, clan *(teip)* and nation, the Chechens are heirs to a tradition of banditry and resistance which has stood them in good stead. Following a series of failed attempts to topple the regime by coups and plots, Moscow was forced to deploy on 11 December 1994 an army equivalent to the initial force which seized Afghanistan in 1979. That invasion had opened a 'bleeding wound' which took the Soviets a decade to staunch. This new intervention similarly marks the beginning of a new and dangerous phase in the disintegration of the Russian empire.

In the interests of administrative efficiency and state control, Stalin arbitrarily merged in 1934 the Chechen and Ingush Autonomous Regions. The Chechens rebelled and, in 1944, the entire people was deported. Over 200 000 died in the process. Resettled and scattered in Central Asia, Siberia and Kazakhstan, the Chechens were only allowed to return to their homeland in 1956. *Perestroika* allowed them to campaign for the autonomy they had so long been denied. The Chechen All National Congress rose to prominence, led by a mercurial former air force general, Dzhokhar Dudayev. Born in 1944, Dudayev had experienced Stalin's resettlement first hand. Although he rose to the rank of major general of aviation, he and his Estonian wife had suffered enough Russian discrimination to leave him with no love for Moscow.

The August Coup in Moscow finally shattered the Union. In Chechen-Ingushetia, Dudayev used the opportunity to overthrow the existing (Soviet) administration, declare independence and call for elections in October 1991; these he duly won. While the Chechens had been a thorn in Gorbachev's side, Yeltsin had tolerated them. Once Dudayev began advocating secession from his new Russian Federation, however, Yeltsin had no more time for him. He declared the election null and void and issued a warrant for Dudayev's arrest, sending a battalion of Russian Interior Troops to enforce it. This proved the true catalyst of Chechen nationhood. The more Moscow inveighed against

Dudayev, the more he became canonized as a hero of national independence. The Interior Troops were blockaded and forced to withdraw. While still legally part of Russia, Chechnya became effectively independent. In December 1992, Ingushetia formally broke away to become a republic on its own within the Russian Federation.

THE CHECHEN *MAFIYA*

One of the factors which gave Chechnya an international significance is that the Chechens have established a multinational criminal network. This includes licit 'upperworld' investments in Germany and the USA, fashionable properties in London and a network of car-thieving, drug trafficking and money laundering stretching across and beyond Eurasia. In part, this is built upon their savagery and loyalty, rooted in a culture with a strong tradition of clan and family discipline and of resistance to external control. One Italian criminal noted that 'where we would first threaten someone, the Russians would kill him. The Chechens would kill his whole family, too.' It also reflected their ability to use Chechnya as a safe haven as well as the Chechen diaspora across Russia, the CIS and, increasingly, the world.

Their wealth, largely derived from frauds and illegal oil trading carried out under the aegis of the Chechen government, allowed the Chechens to move away from direct involvement in the cruder forms of organized crime. Instead, they bankrolled local gangs who, in effect, operated as their 'franchisees'. In addition, the Chechens provided a whole array of financial services to such smaller local groups, such as money laundering and counterfeiting. Their wealth also meant that they have become increasingly involved in 'clean' economic crimes as well as quasi-legal businesses.

Dudayev soon become little more than a figurehead for a dominant coalition of clans and criminal cartels. The new Chechen state was essentially built around established *teips* which also formed the backbone of Chechen organized crime. Consider, for example, the Chechen police force. Having inherited a Soviet system with three main services and 3000 officers, this mushroomed to 14 separate forces, accounting for some 17 000 armed officers.

What had happened was that clans within Dudayev's alliance were simply given the opportunity to turn their gunmen into state law-enforcement officers, albeit still responsible to their clan elders. It was clearly very useful for criminals to have the trappings and respectability of a state. It opened up an entire economy to their plunder. Whereas once only two per cent of Chechnya's oil revenues remained within the region, this officially became 100 per cent. Yet, in the first two years of independence, not a single new

school or hospital was built and industrial production fell by 60 per cent —
largely as a result of under-investment. The criminals could also use their
new positions to exploit outsiders. Thanks to its control of the Chechen State
Bank, one gang was able to use false *avisos* (proof of fund documents) to
defraud the Russian State Bank of currency worth perhaps US$700 million.
In February 1993, two Chechen *mafiosi* were killed while in Britain,
travelling on Chechen diplomatic passports. They were killed by Armenian
assassins who wanted to prevent them from selling missiles to the Azeris for
use in the war between the two countries. Yet their deaths also brought to
light attempts by this nation of counterfeiters to use the good offices of the
British Royal Mint to acquire the latest in currency and documentation
printing technology.

THE PHONEY WAR
On several levels, then, Chechen nationalism represented a problem for
Moscow. It was a haven for organized crime, beyond the reach of Moscow's
law enforcers yet nominally within Russian borders. It was costing the centre
billions in oil revenues withheld and oil stolen from pipelines crossing
Chechen soil. It undermined Moscow's authority in the North Caucasus.
Dudayev was eager to create a federation of the 41 Caucasian *gorskii*
(mountain) peoples in the mould of Imam Shamil, the nineteenth-century
hero and inspiration of the Caucasian wars against the Russians. Although
his Confederation of Caucasian Mountain Peoples never amounted to much,
events in Chechnya did threaten the stability of the region. Three of
Chechnya's 18 constituent regions threatened secession. Dudayev began to
threaten the forced re-incorporation of Ingushetia into his nation. The Terek
Cossack Host laid claim to parts of Chechnya. There appeared ample scope
for unrest, local insurrection, even civil war.

Since mid-1992, Moscow had sought to topple the Dudayev regime. In
the summer of 1994, despite the economic crisis, Yeltsin still managed to find
another 150 billion roubles to intensify the covert war. To an extent, this
policy had little to do with events in Groznyy and much more about power
politics back in Moscow.

With Boris Yeltsin little more than an ailing and failing figurehead,
policy over Chechnya was in the hands of an informal 'kitchen cabinet' of a
handful of grandees driven above all by personal and institutional self-
interests. The prime movers behind the war were four:

■ Major General Alexander Korzhakov, head of the Presidential
Security Service (SBP). A powerful confidante of Yeltsin's, Korzhakov
urged Yeltsin to take a tougher line with his critics. He felt that he was in

a no-lose situation over Chechnya. A prompt victory would rebound to the credit of the internal security forces, including his SBP, while a drawn-out guerrilla war would raise dangers of Chechen terrorism, justifying additional funding for his personal fiefdom.

■ Sergei Stepashin, former director of the Federal Counter-intelligence Service (FSK — *Federal'naya sluzhba kontrrazvedki*). Like Korzhakov, Stepashin felt a success in Chechnya would boost his prestige and that of his service. He was the main organizer of Moscow's initial covert war against Dudayev, funding, arming and organizing the opposition. However, he was forced to resign in late June because of the government's poor handling of the Chechen hostage siege in Budyonnovsk the previous month.

■ Viktor Yerin, former minister of Internal Affairs. The Interior Ministry (MVD) consistently supported the FSK. Yerin needed to re-establish his authority following a rough ride in parliament and also wanted to justify current plans for an expansion of the ministry's paramilitary Interior Troops (VV — *Vnutrennye voiska*). His policemen were also eager to do something about this nest of crime. Yerin also resigned from the government in late June.

■ Nikolai Yegorov, the man later to be nominated Yeltsin's special representative in Chechnya. As Russia's minister for Nationalities and Regional Policy, he staked much upon a confrontational line. Not only did he hail from Krasnodar, a neighbouring Russian region with no love for the Chechens, but he also wanted to win greater public profile and political authority. In the short term, it certainly paid off. Yeltsin's final commitment to military intervention was marked by Yegorov's promotion to the rank of deputy prime minister. Like Stepashin's and Yerin's, though, his career became hostage to developments in Chechnya and he too resigned in late June.

In the autumn of 1994, this so-called 'party of war' launched a private invasion. A ramshackle coalition of Dudayev's opponents was assembled and armed, ranging from democrats to smaller *teips* who had failed to win a place inside his ruling alliance. Stiffened with mercenaries and Russian troops hired by the FSK without the knowledge of their commanders or the Defence Ministry, they launched an attack on Groznyy in November. It failed conclusively but upped the ante considerably. Russian soldiers were captured and publicly admitted their mission, humiliating the defence minister and showing Moscow's hand. The 'phoney war' could no longer be characterized as a domestic Chechen affair. Instead, Moscow either had to prove it had the power to topple Dudayev or face humiliation.

THE DECISION TO INTERVENE
The public failure of the November coup thus made full-scale and open intervention almost inevitable. Not only could the government not afford to lose face but those leaders who had been behind the covert war had also to salvage their own reputations. Plans for the intervention were finalized at a meeting in the border town of Mozdok on 8 December. Present were the Sergei Stepashin, a senior VV commander and Yegorov. Defence Minister Grachev was expected to be present but he failed to appear. His position was, as usual, ambiguous. He had consistently opposed the use of the army in internal operations, most strikingly in October 1993 when Yeltsin had personally to petition him to send his tanks to shell parliament into submission. As a veteran of Afghanistan, he also understood the potential dangers in the ill-conceived invasion of a mountainous Muslim nation. He also knew that the internal security agencies wanted to start and win such a war as part of their campaign to acquire greater budgets and powers. If they could prove that domestic unrest posed a greater threat to the stability and future of the Russian state than external aggression, they could begin to poach monies otherwise intended for the military. After all, it was no coincidence that the escalation of their campaign coincided with discussion of the defence budget in the State Duma. The prize was an extra 15 trillion roubles earmarked for the defence budget, perhaps a third of which the FSK and MVD believed they could hijack. On 6 December, it was announced that only five trillion roubles would automatically go to the Defence Ministry but that the security agencies still needed to prove their case for some of the remaining funds. On 11 December, units of the VV and the army's North Caucasian Military District (SKVO — *Srednyi kavkazskyi voennyi okrug*) entered Chechnya.

Grachev thus sought to avoid war but at every turn he found himself undermined by his lack of authority both in Moscow and within the armed forces as a whole. He personally brokered a ceasefire with Dudayev, which FSK-controlled forces promptly broke. At first, he had refused to contribute army units to the initial invasion forces. The FSK had simply hired soldiers behind his back, while the local commanders of the SKVO appeared happier co-operating with the internal security agencies than the Defence Ministry. In particular, Lieutenant Generals Mityukhin and Potapov, SKVO commander and chief of staff respectively, appear to have become closely allied with the parallel VV command hierarchy in the region. SKVO units were thus involved in the initial operation. First Deputy Defence Minister Boris Gromov was suspended following his first warning that military intervention would be a mistake, a view Grachev shared but did not dare express. Major General Babichev, commander of one element of the invasion forces, refused at one point to press on with an attack on meeting civilian protesters.

To an extent, Grachev's vacillation thus reflected an ambiguity within the armed forces. In the absence of consensus at the centre, much of the initiative passed to individual groups and institutions. Marginalized in Moscow, despised within the officer corps, Grachev proved too weak to resist the official line for long. He was forced to come into line and assemble what units he could to salvage an operation the VV had begun but could not complete. While Grachev had originally stood to gain political capital by his refusal to become involved in the intervention, he now could not win. Not only had he again been shown to lack the resolution to stand his ground, he became involved in a humbling search for units able and willing to participate. In some cases, notionally 'combat ready' elements were shown to lack the resources and discipline to be deployed. In others, commanders refused any part in the force, an increasingly common form of 'passive mutiny' first witnessed during the August Coup in 1991, then again during October 1993. Certain air force units, in particular, simply communicated their refusal to take part in the bombing of Groznyy, while even some VV forces refused deployment to Chechnya.

AN AUDIT OF THE WAR

Russia's blundering invasion of Chechnya represented one of the first opportunities to assess the true capabilities of the new Russian army. It hardly shone. In the face of over 40 000 Russian troops and paramilitaries, the Chechens mustered perhaps 3000 regular soldiers and around 30 000 often badly equipped and disorganized irregulars. Nevertheless, the Russians took over a month to seize Groznyy and, in the process, lost more men than in the initial invasion of Afghanistan in 1979.

In hindsight, it is relatively easy to identify the five main reasons for the Russians' poor showing:

■ **Disunity of the High Command**. Pavel Grachev's term as defence minister has seen one of the most effectively integrated and co-ordinated commands in the world descent into bickering recrimination. The war led to the effective suspension of three deputy defence ministers.

■ **Lack of co-ordination**. The disunity of the High Command was reflected on the ground and the haphazard way the invasion force was put together. Local and central army units, Naval Infantry, special forces, Interior Troops, Border Troops, police paramilitaries and Cossack volunteers were all represented. 'Friendly fire' incidents, where Russians fired on Russians, were commonplace and operations were marked by a distinct lack of effective joint action.

Figure 7.1: The Chechen intervention

1994

3 September	Chechen rebels launch anti-government offensive.
26 November	Chechen rebels attack Groznyy but are defeated.
29 November	Security Council meets to consider measures 'to restore law and order' in Chechnya.
30 November	Yeltsin threatens invasion.
7-9 December	Three Groups of Forces assemble on Chechen border *(see Figure 7.2)*.
9 December	Yeltsin issues Presidential Decree 2166 'On Measures to Disband Illegal Armed Formations on the Territory of the Chechen Republic and into the Area of the Ossetian-Ingush Conflict'.
11 December	Invasion.
17 December	Nikolai Yegorov appointed presidential representative in Chechnya.
23 December	Caucasus Special Border District establishes HQ to seal Chechen borders.
31 December	Assault on Groznyy begins *(see Figure 7.2)*.

1995

6 January	Official casualties: 256 Russians dead.
7 January	Major General Viktor Vorobyov, commander of Internal Troops in Chechnya, killed in Groznyy.
8-12 January	Russian forces reinforced with Interior Troops, marines and paratroopers.
9-11 January	Ceasefire in Groznyy.
19 January	Presidential Palace seized by 276th Motor Rifle Regiment and 876th Independent Assault-Landing Battalion; Generals Gromov, Mironov and Kondratyev, who had all been critical of the war, relieved of their posts.
22 January	Gromov claims that the operation was 'prepared, planned, carried out and run by inept commanders'.
27 January	Yegorov replaced on grounds of ill-health by Nikolai Semyonov.
31 January	Official casualties: 735 Russians dead.
1 February	Interior Troops' commander-in-chief, Colonel General Kulikov, appointed overall commander of Federal Forces in Chechnya.
16 February	Yeltsin defends the invasion to the Duma.
6 March	Moscow claims to have taken control of whole of Groznyy: war moves to the towns and the countryside.

Figure 7.2: Forces involved in the Chechen War

Russian invasion forces

	Commander	Main elements
Northern Group	Lt Gen L Rokhlin	8th Army Corps 131st Independent Motor Rifle Brigade
Southeastern Group	Maj Gen N Staskov	106th Guards Airborne Division 56th Indep Airborne Brigade
Western Group	Maj Gen I Babichev	76th Guards Airborne Division 19th Motor Rifle Division 21st Independent Airborne Brigade

In total: 38 000 troops, 230 tanks, 454 AFVs.

Russian forces involved in the Battle for Groznyy

- 74th Independent Motor Rifle Brigade.
- 129th Motor Rifle Regiment of the 45th Motor Rifle Division.
- 81st Motor Rifle Regiment of the 90th Tank Division.
- 276th Motor Rifle Regiment of the 34th Motor Rifle Division.
- Interior Troop forces.

Regular Chechen forces

These units were given grandiose titles but tended to comprise only a few hundred soldiers under a charismatic commander. They totalled less than 3000.

- Motorized Brigade — actually little more than a company, with 200 men.
- Shali Tank Regiment — 200 men, with 15 combat-ready tanks.
- Commando Brigade — a light motorized force, 300 men.
- Artillery Regiment — 200 men, with 30 light and medium guns.
- National Guard (sometimes picturesquely described as the 'Kamikaze Regiment') — along with the other forces subordinated directly to the president, including the 'Muslim Hunter Regiment' and the 'Abkhaz Battalion', perhaps 1000 fighters in total.
- Ministry of Internal Affairs' Regiment — 200 men.
- Chechen Air Force — a dozen combat-ready aircraft, mostly L-15 trainers.

Irregular Chechen forces

In many cases these were village militias or clan gunmen who had been nominally enrolled into the police as a way for the government to grant them licences to carry weapons. They numbered perhaps 30 000.

- Self-Defence Units — village militias.
- Patrol-Guard Service — police.

■ **A failure to apply the new military doctrine**. In theory, the Russian army should have been ready for such an operation. Not only could it draw on the experiences of Afghanistan but also the new military doctrine approved in 1993 dwelt on such low-intensity conflicts (*see Chapter 3*). In practice, though, the elite forces prepared for such a mission were reluctant to get involved and thus the Russians relied on their traditional mainstays: artillery, force of numbers and terror tactics. Tellingly, one of the deputy defence ministers sacked for his resistance to the war was Colonel General Boris Gromov, the last commander of Soviet forces in Afghanistan.

■ **Low morale and combat readiness**. Few Russian soldiers had any great enthusiasm for the war. Indeed, cases of desertions or of commanders refusing to send their men to Chechnya were commonplace. Basic Russian combat tradecraft was equally poor, even in notionally elite units.

■ **Chechen tactics and fighting spirit**. In contrast to the Russians, the Chechens made the most of what they had. During the nineteenth-century wars of Russian conquest, they won a name for their dogged and deadly defence of their homelands. Today's Chechens maintained that proud tradition. That also meant that Dudayev, contrary to some Russians' expectations, could not be counted on to cut a deal. As soon as Russian forces began the operation, Dudayev lost all room for manoeuvre. His personal position, which had been shaky, was bolstered but became entirely dependent upon his anti-Russian stance. Concessions would bring the danger of being outflanked by Islamic extremists, from the Turkish Grey Wolves to the Afghan mojaheddin, who came to Chechnya both to fight Russia and to campaign for a strict Islamic state.

PROSPECTS FOR THE FUTURE

Whatever the reasons for failure, the war cannot be characterized as anything but. In its first four months, it cost the Russians the lives of over 1000 troops. It also created 370 000 refugees. Early estimates put the cost of the war at 3.5 trillion roubles; given that the first four months cost 1.9 trillion roubles, this is probably conservative as the reconstruction of Chechnya will take years. At this rate, the extra five trillion roubles the security agencies hoped to squeeze out of an already overstretched budget will scarcely meet the cost of the war they engineered. Intervention also radicalized opinion amongst the other *gorskii* peoples and further tarnished the Yeltsin regime. It also led to domestic complications, not least in the southern Russian town of Budyonnovsk. In June 1995, Chechen guerrillas proved able to bypass, bribe and bluff their way past numerous security controls to seize over 2500 hostages. Fighting off two attempts to storm the hospital which they had occupied, they then proceeded to negotiate safe passage back home and an at least temporary cessation of hostilities. The war really had come home to the Russians.

Moscow's latest Caucasian war thus has four main implications for the rest of the world:

■ **It is undermining the Yeltsin regime**. This comes at a time when there is no clear replacement for him. Until recently, Boris Yeltsin's personal commitment to democratization — however idiosyncratic — was one of the few guarantees the outside world had that Russia was genuinely changing. This can hardly still be the case. The main beneficiaries are the internal security agencies which are, if anything, rolling back attempts to establish the institutional and legal bases for democracy. Prospects of Chechen terrorism are already being used to justify even greater security budgets and yet more draconian laws. Pretexts have been found to oust the few remaining liberals within the agencies, such as former Moscow FSK chief Yevgeni Savostyanov. In the words of Yegor Gaidar, 'War means bigger military spending, a state of emergency across Russia and, finally, the introduction of a police state. In other words, an attack on Groznyy means the death of Russia's democracy tomorrow.' The Russian media's preparedness to use its new democratic freedoms and inform the public of the reality behind the government propaganda has further undermined the regime's legitimacy and even led to worrying a campaign to restore the old machinery of censorship.

■ **The attempt to assert Moscow's control has backfired**. Dudayev's authority in Chechnya has been reasserted and his hitherto empty rhetoric about a North Caucasian *gorskii* confederation has been given new legitimacy. Other non-Russian regions within the Federation, from Tatarstan to Udmurtia, have begun to reconsider both the virtue of remaining under Moscow's control and, more ominously, the centre's ability to defend its hegemony. It is not surprising, after all, that Moscow could ultimately capture Groznyy. What is surprising is how long it took the Russians and how inconclusive was their victory.

■ **The coherence and discipline of the armed forces have been further undermined**. Grachev failed to stand up to the clique running Russia and instead plunged half-heartedly and unprepared into the intervention. Individual officers and units have been able to flout his orders with impunity. What respect and authority can Grachev and his ministry still command?

■ **An operation intended to crush a stronghold of overt criminality will actually contribute to the integration of global organized crime.** Within the strange and shadowy ecology of global crime, the Chechens preyed upon and controlled their Russian counterparts. The war in Chechnya will lead to purges and realignments within the Chechen underworld which will halt and maybe reverse its expansion. This will open up new opportunities for its Russian counterparts. One way in which the Chechens are distinctive is that, unlike the ethnic Russian gangs, they have shown little inclination to co-operate with established criminal associations. They thus buck the trend towards the global integration of international crime which has seen alliance between the US and European mafias and the Colombian gangs, and which is increasingly incorporating Russian groups into a trans-national cartel. The Chechens' losses will thus be the gains of those Russian gangs which have cultivated stronger ties with existing groups, such as the Sicilian mafia. This will be a step further in the increasing co-operation within, and integration of, global organized crime.

■ **It raises doubts as to how far Moscow can be trusted by the outside world.** The operation has highlighted very real doubts as to whether the Russians can be seen as a reliable partners (*see Chapter 9*). Policy appears to be decided by small cabals of conspirators rather than through any legitimate and accountable institutions. Besides, much of what Moscow has done violates the letter or spirit of many international understandings.

In 1904, Russian Interior Minister Plehve advocated hostilities with Japan. 'A nice victorious little war' was, he felt, just what Russia needed to regain its cohesion and self-esteem. Disaster in the Russo-Japanese War brought tsarist Russia the 1905 revolutions, international contempt and bankruptcy. History repeated is, after all, either tragedy or farce.

8 Big Brother: Russia and the 'Near Abroad'

Russia has never been prepared to accept a passive role in Eurasia. Instead, Russian strategists through the ages have interpreted the country's history in a way which supports their view that it is only by a proactive and, ultimately, ruthlessly pragmatic policy that the security of this sprawling multi-ethnic land empire can be assured. Thus, Tsar Nicholas I sent his troops into Europe during the revolutions of the 1840s not on missions of conquest but to restore ousted autocrats and thus maintain a conservative status quo. Stalin, by contrast, looked to a 'strategic glacis' of puppet states to protect his empire from the ideological contagion and perceived military threat from the West. Even sluggish Brezhnev would invade Czechoslovakia in 1968 and Afghanistan in 1979 and rattle sabres on Poland's borders in 1980-81, all to preserve the USSR's regional hegemony.

Isolationism and passivity have thus never been regarded as credible options for Russia. If anything, after all, Russia's position and future are more uncertain now than at any time since 1945. Factionalism is tearing at the government just as regionalism is eating at the unity of the Russian state. The armed forces are in crisis, organized crime is rife and neo-fascist demagogues such as Vladimir Zhirinovsky have cultivated a limited but potentially dangerous constituency demanding the assertion of Moscow's regional interests.

Across Russia's 58 000 km of border are the 15 new nations of what Moscow now calls *blizhnee zarubezhnyi*, the 'Near Abroad'. Many are unstable and most bear long-standing grudges towards her. At stake is the whole map of Eurasia, the whole definition of what the new men in the Kremlin regard as *nash* (ours).

Very broadly speaking, the Russians divide the new nations of the former USSR into four main camps:

■ **The Baltic states: neighbours.** For many reasons, the Baltic states never really fitted into the Soviet mould. Conquered relatively recently (ie during the Second World War), with strong local cultures and

Country	Area (000 km^2)	Population (millions)	Indigenous (%)	Capital	Culture	Economy	Stability
Russia	17 075	147.4	82	Moscow	Slavic Orthodox	Heavy industry, raw materials, petrochemicals, natural gas	Adequate; civil war in Chechnya
Ukraine	604	51.7	73	Kiev	Slavic: mix of Orthodox and Catholic	Heavy industry, agriculture, raw materials	Adequate
Belarus	208	10.2	78	Minsk	Slavic Orthodox (some Polish Catholic)	Heavy industry, agriculture	Good
Moldova	34	4.3	64	Chisinau (Kishinev)	Mainly Romanian Orthodox; some Russian	Some industry, agricultural products (including grapes and wine)	Sporadic civil war
Georgia	70	5.4	70	Tbilisi	Orthodox	Mixed industry, some agriculture	Civil wars
Armenia	30	3.3	93	Yerevan	Orthodox	Some medium industry	Cooling war with Azerbaijan
Azerbaijan	87	7	83	Baku	Islam	Petrochemicals and associated industries	Poor; cooling war with Armenia
Kazakhstan	2717	16.5	42	Almaty (Alma Ata)	Russian Orthodox north, Islamic Kazakh south	Minerals, electricity, agriculture	Fragile; risk of north/south split
Kyrgyzstan	199	4.3	52	Bishkek	Islam	Coal, metals, agriculture	Adequate
Tajikistan	143	5.1	65	Dushanbe	Islam	Cotton and textiles	Very poor; civil war
Turkmenistan	488	3.5	73	Ashkhabad	Islam	Petrochemicals	Adequate
Uzbekistan	447	19.9	71	Tashkent	Islam	Cotton, chemicals	Poor; recent insurrections
Estonia	45	1.6	62	Tallinn	Protestant; large Russian minority	Relatively high-tech light industry; wood, fisheries, agriculture	Relatively good
Latvia	65	2.7	52	Riga	Protestant; large Russian minority	Relatively high-tech light industry; fisheries	Relatively good
Lithuania	65	3.9	80	Vilnius	Catholic	Mixed industry, agriculture	Relatively good

Figure 8.1: The successor states

economies, they have broken most with the old Soviet ways. In this, they have been encouraged by West European and Scandinavian nations eager to help them rejoin a community of European nations. Russia has interests in the Baltic, not least because of the large populations of ethnic Russian settlers and land links with the enclave of Kaliningrad. Moscow does not, however (or yet), see Estonia, Latvia and Lithuania as part of her direct sphere of influence.

■ **Central Asia, Transcaucasia and Moldova: clients.** Russia has capitalized upon the wars and rebellions dividing these nations. By supporting different factions at different times and by judicious economic and military pressure, Armenia, Azerbaijan, Georgia and Moldova have all been forced to accept the presence of Russian troops on their soil. With the possible exception of Azerbaijan, which still hopes to exploit its oil reserves to buy its way out of dependence upon Russia, all have come to accept Moscow's hegemony. Much the same is true in Central Asia, especially in Tajikistan where Russian troops are buttressing a friendly government in a war beginning to look a little like a new Afghanistan.

■ **Belarus: friend.** The election of President Lukashenka in 1994 has led to an ever-closer alliance between Belarus and Russia. Not only does Belarus share very close cultural ties with its fellow Orthodox Slav neighbour but also the government in Minsk is largely made up of Soviet-era leaders with no great enthusiasm for nationalist excess. In addition, they have a keen awareness that they need Moscow's resources and markets for their own projects of national reconstruction.

■ **Ukraine: rival?** Moscow's relations with Ukraine are in many ways the most complex and important. While Ukraine is predominantly populated (73 per cent) by those culturally recognized as 'Ukrainians', the 11.4 million 'Russians' are concentrated in the east of the country and in the Crimea. There, they represent over two-thirds of the population. Crimea is also a heavily fortified region with military installations at Simferopol, Feodosiya and, especially, Sevastopol, home of another bone of contention, namely the former Soviet Black Sea Fleet. While dwarfed by its neighbour, Ukraine is the only nation able to challenge or resist Russian hegemony in Eurasia. Military intervention in Ukraine would not be like the shadow wars fought in Georgia, Moldova and Tajikistan. It would be a proper war, against a Ukrainian army now heavily recruited from the west and equipped with some of the most advanced materiel of the old Soviet forces. After all, the Tashkent Accord of 1992 on dividing Soviet assets entitled Ukraine to 4080 tanks compared to Russia's 6400 (west of the Urals).

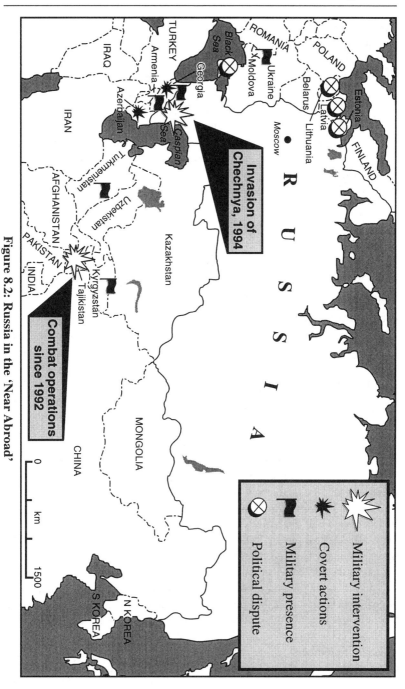

Figure 8.2: Russia in the 'Near Abroad'

Invasion of Chechnya, 1994

Combat operations since 1992

Military intervention
Covert actions
Military presence
Political dispute

THE CIS: UNION OR EMPIRE?

Originally formed in 1991 as part of Boris Yeltsin's campaign to humble Mikhail Gorbachev and partition the USSR, the Commonwealth of Independent States (CIS) was little more than a hollow fiction for its first three years. Attempts to give it a role in economic co-operation foundered on short-sighted national self-interest and generalized financial anarchy. Hopes that it could protect the rights of minorities proved little more than pious rhetoric. Furthermore, suggestions that it could establish a consensual collective security architecture were overtaken by Russia's preparedness to hijack the notion of 'peacekeeping' to legitimize its cross-border interventions. In late 1994, though, the CIS began something of a comeback. As the region's economies slowly began to stabilize, they came to need some new structures to manage and promote intra-regional trade. Russia had also campaigned to convince its neighbours that they could neither compete with Russia nor exist and thrive in opposition to it. In late October, the leaders of all 12 member nations agreed to establish an Inter-State Economic Committee (MEK — *Mezhdunarodnyi ekonomicheskii komitet*). This supranational agency would be charged with furthering economic co-operation within the CIS, to create an 'Eurasian common market'.

Eurasia is hardly Western Europe, however. For all their practical and specific differences, the states of the European Union (EU) share core values, expectations and ambitions that underpin any political co-operation. The CIS, though, is made up of states of wildly differing political outlooks, including two — Armenia and Azerbaijan — officially still at war. They are far from stable and over them looms the shadow of Russia. The EU has its stronger and weaker nations but nothing like the disproportion evident in the CIS. Without firm principles of sovereignty and consensus to ensure that the strong do not steamroller the weak, the result is not a union but an informal empire.

Russia has certainly not been coy in using its military and economic muscle to dominate the new CIS. Symbolically, the MEK was sited in Moscow and votes within it are directly pegged to the share of costs borne. Russia covers half the MEK's costs and buys half its votes. Adding the vote of its ally and neighbour Belarus, and the all-but-client state of Tajikistan, Moscow already has a permanent majority — not that there is much the other nations of the CIS can do. After all, they mistrust but need Russia. They need it as an economic partner, especially as a market and source of raw materials or power. In some cases, they need it as a security partner, sometimes against forces Moscow could otherwise support or encourage. The Abkhazians and Ossetians in Georgia, for example, or the Dniester separatists in Moldova, are smouldering embers which Russia can fan at any time to exert political pressure. Well aware of its strength, Russia is seeking to capitalize upon it for all it is worth, linking its neighbours to itself by ties of economic, military or social dependency.

'NEW IMPERIALISM': RUSSIAN ATTITUDES TOWARDS EURASIA

Russia has adopted an ever-more pragmatic and forward policy to maintain her internal and regional security while imposing a hegemony upon the other states sometimes characterized as the 'New Imperialism'. In some cases, Moscow can rely upon the free market and its economic strength to secure its regional hegemony. At other times, political haggling dominates, while covert pressure and military interventionism occasionally appear beneath the mantle of 'peacekeeping'. Russia has wrapped together concepts such as peacekeeping, regional and collective security, and military assistance with economic interest and traditional interests in a new notion of national security. Embracing not just the security of Russia's borders but also her internal stability and economic interests, this is rooted in a belief that the states of the former Soviet Union are all part of Russia's legitimate — indeed, indispensable — sphere of influence. To the Russians, this is the 'Near Abroad', in contrast to the 'Far Abroad' of China, Europe, the Middle East and beyond. The imperial notion draws its strength from five main wellsprings:

■ **Ethnic interpenetration.** Centuries of empire have left national boundaries bearing little relation to ethnic distribution. There are some 20 million ethnic Russians outside her borders. These communities offer a ready pretext for involvement in neighbouring countries' domestic politics. They are also a constraint — no government in Moscow can afford to ignore their interests. In addition, Russia herself is host to a wide range of ethnic groups. They will inevitably be affected by events outside Russia, whether the rise of Islam to the south or growing tensions between Russian and Ukrainian communities in Ukraine. Thus, there can be no hard and fast divide between domestic and foreign politics.

■ **Economic interdependence.** The economies of the Soviet republics were planned for interdependence, and the fragmentation of the USSR has not so much created 16 new economies as 16 jigsaw pieces of the old. Most are unable to compete effectively in the international market, just as they lack the resources to buy all they want and need and are thus forced into economic co-operation. From Moscow's perspective, Russian hegemony not only facilitates such co-operation but also ensures that it operates to her advantage, allowing her to use her size to dominate the regional economy.

■ **Security interests.** Russia's new military doctrine explicitly locates her security interests not simply at her borders but in all Eurasia. Even peacekeeping operations in the 'Near Abroad' assume a direct security dimension. They not only limit potentially contagious instability on Russian borders but also forestall the intervention of other nations and powers (including the UN) within Russia's self-proclaimed sphere of influence.

■ **Political culture.** Modern Russia is not merely having to create new institutions of statehood, it is having to establish a whole new national identity, a culture of statehood. In part, this is building on and reinforcing traditional Russian attitudes, including a deep-rooted sense of national mission; this also turns into racism when Russians start talking of Central Asians and Caucasians.

■ **Sectional interests.** There are individuals and interest groups standing to gain from the 'New Imperialism'. For Boris Yeltsin, it allows him to steal the clothes of his nationalism rivals — most notably, Vladimir Zhirinovsky. For the Defence Ministry, a more interventionist doctrine represents both a new mission as protector of the Russian diaspora and an argument for sustained funding.

RUSSIAN OPERATIONS IN THE 'NEAR ABROAD'

Moscow certainly does not lack economic and political means with which to exert its influence within the 'Near Abroad'. It has also turned to more direct pressure. Since 1994, it has increasingly used deniable third parties and auxiliary forces. To put pressure on the Georgian government, Ossetian and Abkhazian partisans were armed and sheltered. Armed Cossacks, with implicit sanction from Moscow, supported Slavs in Moldova, the Caucasus and Yugoslavia, and were also a vocal lobby for intervention in Chechnya. One reason for Kazakh President Nazarbaev's conciliatory attitude towards Moscow is the ethnic Russian majority in the north of his country and a fear that they could be used as fifth columnists.

More overt Russian military operations in the 'Near Abroad' have tended to be designated 'peacekeeping operations', although differing widely in scale, purpose and legitimacy. Part of the problem is that Russian perceptions of 'peacekeeping' are very different from those of the West. For a start, they use two distinct expressions:

■ **'Operations in support of peace'** *(Operatsii po poderzhaniyu mira)* are essentially similar to Western notions of 'peacekeeping'. They involve limited military interventions following on from political agreements brokered on the ground. Such actions are usually confined to maintaining UN-style 'green lines', keeping belligerents apart and monitoring compliance with cease-fire and demilitarization accords.

■ **'Peacemaking operations'** *(Mirotvorcheskiye operatsii)*, on the other hand, involve the use of force to separate warring parties and impose Moscow's writ. In Tajikistan, for example, Russian forces have been engaged in battalion-level operations, with full air and artillery support, fought as a military attack rather than under the rules and conditions of peacekeeping.

A second distinction which needs to be drawn between different operations relates to the authority on which they draw. Some, for example, follow multinational agreements, concluded without duress and legitimized by the terms of the CIS charter (in particular, collective security accords signed at Tashkent Summit in July 1992). In other cases, though, Moscow has simply arrogated upon herself the right to intervene to protect Russian nationals or Russian borders. In cases such as the deployment of Russian troops in Georgia in 1994, the invitation issued by Tbilisi was nothing more than the skimpiest pretext and followed sustained pressure from Moscow.

The upsurge in nationalism associated with the collapse of the USSR had, after all, led to particular tensions between the Georgians on the one hand, and the Ossetian minorities to the north of the country and Abkhazian minorities to the west on the other. In December 1990, the Ossetians took up arms against the government, seeking to be united with their cousins across the border in southern Russia. By July 1992, nearly 2000 had died in the conflict. That month a joint force of Russian and Georgian soldiers and Russian Ossetians was introduced, controlling local tensions. Further Russian interventions in Georgia proved less benign, though. In 1994, the refusal of Georgian President Shevardnadze to join the CIS and make political concessions to Moscow led to covert support being provided to anti-government forces, including the rebellious Abkhazian peoples of the west. Shevardnadze was forced to capitulate: Georgia joined the CIS, accepted a long-term role for the 2500-strong Russian 'peacekeeping' contingent in Abkhazia and granted Moscow the right to station troops in three bases.

By contrast, Russian involvement in Moldova, following the secession of the 'Dniester Republic', has taken two, apparently distinct, forms. The 14th Army, garrisoned in the region, to a large extent took upon itself the task of defending the Slav rebels rather than the legitimate government in Chisinau (Kishinev). While in late 1994 an agreement was signed between Moscow and Chisinau to withdraw the 14th Army, its three-year span gives ample room for manoeuvre and renegotiation. In addition, a joint peacekeeping force was introduced in July 1992; it was made up of 1500 Russian troops as well as Moldovan and 'Dniester Republic' forces. These have largely been deployed in a generally successful effort to maintain a ceasefire along the

Dniester river. By implicitly accepting the rebels' claim to sovereignty, the force is protecting them. That same year, Russian forces became involved in Tajikistan. In April 1992, civil war erupted between the standing regime of President Rakhmon Nabiyev and a coalition of opposition forces dominated by Islamic fundamentalists. The Russians feared the collapse of a friendly government and mistrusted the opposition's links with Afghan extremist factions. They established a joint CIS peacekeeping force under the pretext of protecting non-Tajiks in the republic. The new government found itself torn between pragmatic and fundamentalist wings, though. In November, it appealed again for Russian assistance in the face of renewed civil war and a growth in the number of fighters crossing the border with Afghanistan. Russia's 201st Motor Rifle Division became the core of a 20 000-strong intervention force which, as of mid-1995, seems destined for a lengthy stay. Here, 'peacekeeping' really means supporting a friendly government — some have characterized it as little more than a puppet regime — against rebels whose activities could undermine regional stability and the underpinnings of Russian security on its southern borders.

Alongside direct military intervention have been Russian efforts to use political pressure to further its regional interests. In 1992-93, this was largely directed against the Baltic states but 1994 saw a shift in focus. Arm's-length support for the Russian community in Crimea, for example, led to problems for the Ukrainian government throughout 1994. Kiev, after all, is aware that too sharp a confrontation with the Crimea might prompt a response from Moscow as well as other Russian communities in the east of the country. On the other hand, it cannot appear unable to stamp its authority upon the peninsula. Russia's role in the long-running war between Armenia and Azerbaijan has also been both ambitious and ambiguous. In 1993, it supported the overthrow of Abulfaz Elichibey's pro-Turkish regime with a much more friendly government. At different times, Moscow has supported first one side then the other, to an extent to keep the war running and exhaust both sides. By 1994, Russia was offering to help broker and police an end to the war. This would not only help stabilize her whole southern flank but also allow Moscow to stamp her military and political authority on the region. By the end of 1994, the Russians had established two bases in Armenia.

SOME CONCLUSIONS: A FRAGILE DREAM OF EMPIRE
Russian hegemony over the territories of the 'Near Abroad' has largely been established but may prove fragile. The steady expansion of Russian influence is certainly not irreversible and will involve a further outstretching of Moscow's arm. This is, by no means yet, a new Eurasian 'Warsaw Pact'.

Russia certainly lacks the old USSR's military preponderance. In addition, Soviet control over Central and Eastern Europe was exercised through not only military and economic muscle but also local Party structures with a stake in the status quo. These structures had been infiltrated into all sectors of political life during the period of Soviet occupation during and after the Second World War. Lacking such local agents, Russian regional hegemony needs regularly to be reaffirmed, whether by proof of the economic advantage in alliance with Moscow or through military pressure. The economic factor may become less important in time, putting ever greater emphasis upon military authority.

Yet Russian military intervention is already over-stretching her resources. Russia cannot maintain her present level of commitment, much less develop the forces she needs to impose lasting military hegemony over Eurasia. Most Russian units are under-manned, undisciplined and demoralized, bereft of a clear role and identity and inadequately housed, trained and equipped. Intervention forces, though, need to be trained, supplied and motivated to superior levels, all of which takes both money and political will. Russian state finances cannot continue to maintain the existing level of commitment, though, and ultimately Russian military aspirations will have to be reduced.

Russians are, after all, unlikely to be prepared to bear the ultimate costs of 'New Imperialism'. In part, the new assertiveness of Russian policy in the 'Near Abroad' has been ascribed to populism and the rise of extremists such as Zhirinovsky. Weighed down by economic and social disruption and revolution, reeling at the loss of their world role and, indeed, of their familiar Soviet state, the Russians certainly like to be told of their genetic greatness, of their spiritual mandate. In practice, though, an empire must be bought with money, blood and discipline, and there is no evidence to suggest any general willingness on the part of the Russians to make such sacrifices.

While the future may well thus see further manifestations of 'New Imperialism', there must also come an increasing realism. Russia must once again redefine her genuine security interests and the stage upon which she must act. Attention will shift to the domestic problems of what one could call the 'New Abroad', whether quelling rebellious Caucasian clansmen or convincing sober Far Eastern local authorities that their future lies with Moscow and not greater independence. The price of tsarist and Soviet dreams of empire proved to be bankruptcy and collapse; the new Russia is unlikely to be prepared to risk the same fate. After all, the largely artificial and unstable division of the old USSR into new 'nations' provides no end of divided loyalties, disputed territories and casi belli. Post-colonial Africa has shown the problems which arise when political units do not reflect communities or ethnic groupings in a climate of scarcity and hardship. The current boundaries of the successor states themselves largely reflect the ill-advised or actively mischievous policies of tsarist and Soviet imperialists. Central Asian republics were created simply as useful administrative units. Khrushchev handed Crimea to the Ukrainian leadership in 1954 as a reward for their political support. Stalin relocated entire nationalities to open up new lands or tighten internal security. Consequently, there is a real need for rationalization. Yet, who could even attempt such a task? The UN is not about to start redrawing the boundaries of member nations, even should those states request it. The CIS lacks the power and the legitimacy. Even when it does act, it largely repeats the mistakes of the old USSR, controlling nationalism but without solving the underlying disputes. Perhaps history will have to be played out in full — bloody and prolonged — as it is elsewhere, from Rwanda to Yugoslavia.

9   From Second World to Third: Russia's Global Role?

The rather unlikely truth about modern Russian foreign policy is that it has its roots in a debate of the last century between Russian artists, radicals, conservatives and philosophers. At issue was the vexed question of just what sort of country was Russia and what sort of country should it be. At one extreme were Westernizers who saw Russia as a backward nation which should strive to catch up with, and emulate, the advanced powers of Europe. The more conservative Slavophiles, by contrast, saw Russia's as a distinct society and polity. Her position between Asia and Europe was something in which to glory and exploit rather than be ashamed about. This dialogue was revived and given direct relevance in the 1990s in the debate between the 'Atlanticists' and the 'Eurasians'. The 'Atlanticists' were ardent Westernizers and reformists who stood four-square for radical marketization of the economy, wholehearted collaboration with the West and a total break with Russia's Soviet and tsarist past. The 'Eurasians', instead, warned that Russia's interests were not necessarily those of the West. To an extent this was a very negative point of view, founded on a suspicion of former Cold War rivals and a fear that over-hasty economic and political reform would tear the country apart. It was also a positive creed, though, suggesting that there were aspects of Russia's history, position and society worth preserving and developing. In foreign policy terms, this manifested itself as a wariness of the West and a desire instead to maintain some balance between Europe and Asia, between co-operation and caution.

Within a few years, the waning radicalism of the Yeltsin regime saw the triumph of the 'Eurasians' in foreign policy. Little illustrates this better than the evolution of Foreign Minister Kozyrev's views. Andrei Kozyrev had become for many the embodiment of the 'Atlanticist' platform. He had even been born in Brussels to a diplomatic family, and his reformist pedigree was impeccable. He studied at the liberal Moscow State Institute for Foreign Relations (MGIMO), he had been an aide to Foreign Minister Shevardnadze from 1985 and he was appointed as Yeltsin's foreign minister in 1990. With his Western suits and Western ways, Kozyrev was a high-profile apostle of the 'Atlanticist' line. He played a key role in ensuring that Moscow supported the Western allies in their war against Iraq in 1991. By 1993, Yeltsin's views were changing, however. Put to the test of his convictions, Kozyrev chose to hang on to his job, instead. Relations were re-opened with Iraq and the PLO. Moscow began to champion the Slav Serbs in Yugoslavia and conniving at the smuggling of guns and mercenaries to support them. By 1995, he was even making a case for gunboat diplomacy and defying the West over the expansion of NATO eastwards and the sale of nuclear reactors to Iran.

MOVERS AND SHAKERS

In many ways, Kozyrev is the advocate of Russian foreign policy, not its shaper. The actual process at work is a murky and confused one, centring on the battle to win the ear and heart of President Yeltsin. One of the things making Russian foreign policy often so difficult to predict is the variety of groups and individuals with a say in its formulation and the different interests at work:

■ **The president.** The Russian constitution grants the president a dominant say in foreign policy, with powers ranging from the right to declare and end wars to the appointment of ambassadors. Boris Yeltsin has used his authority sporadically, largely allowing himself to be swayed by advisers and situations.

■ **The prime minister.** Constitutionally, the prime minister has fairly limited competence in the field of international relations. All the same, Viktor Chernomyrdin has asserted his right to a say. His view is, quite correctly, that Russian foreign policy must first and foremost be directed towards assisting domestic policy. As a result, he has been especially active in promoting economic diplomacy and seeking foreign aid and expertise.

■ **The Ministry of Foreign Affairs.** The fortunes of the Foreign Ministry have waxed and waned with those of Kozyrev. As he turned his back on the 'Atlanticist' line, Yeltsin has regained the Kremlin's traditional suspicion of career diplomats. Increasingly, the Foreign Ministry is thus seen as an executive arm and a source of primary information rather than a force for active decision-making. This may change if, as is rumoured, Yeltsin replaces Kozyrev with a closer political ally.

■ **The military.** Although the defence minister himself is politically weak, the armed forces have not been backward about expressing their views on issues that they think are at the heart of national security. Over arms treaties, for example, they have tried to persuade the government to revise those agreed during the Soviet era and which they feel are no longer in Russia's interests. In this, they have been largely unsuccessful but their resistance to any transfer of the disputed far eastern Kurile islands to Japan has, to date, prevented the government from making any such gesture in a bid to woo Tokyo.

■ **The Security Services.** Russia's security and intelligence services have traditionally played a more active role in formulating foreign policy than in the West and this remains the case. Compared with the days of the KGB, though, their interventions are less decisive, largely because there are now so many, each with their own interests and agendas *(see Chapter 11)*. The Federal Security Service (FSB), for example, which is responsible for counter-intelligence, has adopted a hawkish line. Accusations of increased Western spying, after all, reinforce its claim for a greater budget. The Tax Police (NP — *Nalogovaya politsiya*), by contrast, are all too well aware that it is their task to trace much of the revenue which flows into and through European and North American banks. Thus, they would like closer relations and thus greater co-operation.

■ **Economic interests.** Given the close links between politicians and business, economic interests also have an important role in the process, albeit one which is hard to define given the very number of such lobbies. A particular problem is the extent to which many government agencies, starved of state funds, are having to operate as commercial bodies to survive. It was an alliance between the arms dealing cartel Rosvooruzheniye and Minatom, the Ministry of Atomic Energy, which stiffened the government's resolve to resist US pressure and go ahead with a deal to supply nuclear power stations to Iran in 1995. With debts in excess of 2.5 trillion roubles, Minatom needed the sale, while Rosvooruzheniye feared it would lose its traditional markets in the developing world if Russia no longer seemed a reliable partner.

■ **Parliament.** The Duma has very little real responsibility for foreign policy. It has a relevant committee which examines the policies and their execution and issues regular reports but it has no actual power.

■ **Local authorities and prancing proconsuls.** Given the general decentralization of power in today's Russia, it is hardly surprising that local authorization should also apply to international contacts, especially over economic co-operation. By extension, all sorts of other individuals, interests groups and loose cannons are playing a part in shaping Russia's foreign relations. The Cossacks, for example, are not merely a lobby for a more assertive role in the 'Near Abroad' but have also taken a strong position on the retention of lands in the Far East due to be ceded to China and Japan.

Given the range of actors concerned, it is perhaps surprising to note just how successful much of Russian foreign policy has been. There has been no large-scale aid programme but there never was much practical likelihood of that. At least there are organizations such as the European Bank of Reconstruction and Development (EBRD) and projects such as the British 'Know-How Fund' to provide sensible targeted assistance. Russia has managed to retain much of the trappings of Soviet superpower, such as its permanent seat on the UN Security Council, without sacrificing much freedom of manoeuvre. It has still been able to destabilize neighbouring countries, bomb Groznyy to rubble, sell Iran nuclear technology and generally act as it pleases without significant sanction. Internal opposition was one of the main stumbling blocks to incorporating the nations of Central and Eastern Europe into NATO, even though there was no moral or legal rationale why Moscow should think it had, or deserved, the right to say with whom Poland or Estonia should ally. The reason for this is that there is, after all, a certain and subtle power in weakness. With so many Western leaders — and Bill Clinton, in particular — having staked their Russian policies upon Boris Yeltsin's administration, they have felt they could not risk destabilizing him. For a long time, the Soviet Union's foreign relations depended on bluff, given its relative bankruptcy and backwardness. That is a lesson and an art apparently not lost in the Kremlin.

THE VIEW WEST: CAN RUSSIA BE A PARTNER?
Consider, for instance, the 'Partnership for Peace' (PfP) initiative which NATO promulgated at its January 1994 summit. It represented an ambitious bid to lock Russia into a virtuous circle of confidence-building while reassuring nervous Central and East European nations with a commitment short of full NATO membership. It would do more than just provide a forum for East/West dialogue and consultation. The initiative also provided incentives for Russia to move closer to its liberal capitalist neighbours. While the nations of Central and Eastern Europe, as well as Ukraine and Moldova, rushed to sign the PfP, Russia's position remained ambiguous, however.

The programme, while ostensibly welcoming Russia, was also clearly predicated upon widespread fears of her expansionism. Beyond knee-jerk fears that it was part of creeping Western imperialism, there were genuine concerns as to whether the PfP would be — in the long term — in Russia's national interest. After all, the quid pro quo is to be found in a limited exchange of Russia's freedom to extend her interests and authority within her environs in return for Western support, a new level of international legitimacy and an exchange of ideas and consultation. At the moment, though, Russia's national interest is still defined by two interlinked, yet ultimately irreconcilable, concerns — whether her future lies with the West or outside it. On the one hand, there is clear material advantage in closer links with the North Atlantic community. The majority of Russia's foreign trade and investment comes from the West. These nations also dominate the international structures, from the EBRD and G7 to the UN, through which Moscow hopes to find the resources for the reconstruction of the country. Russia also benefits from its ability to exploit its new relationship with the West. Far from being unscrupulous imperialists, Moscow's former rivals have shown themselves very cautious in their dealings with Russia, forever concerned not to undermine Boris Yeltsin's position or provide ammunition for nationalists of the Zhirinovsky school. Russia has shown itself prepared to use this latitude and restraint. In Yugoslavia, for example, Moscow managed to pose as international peacemaker while supporting its Serbian allies. The West sat back and let it bully Eduard Shevardnadze into joining the CIS and 'inviting' Russian troops in to Georgia. In the longer term, though, Russian and Western security interests look set to diverge. It may also limit hopes of establishing Russia as a distinct Eurasian power, able to play off the West against the rising Pacific Rim. Russia's relations with China, in particular, remain one of the great imponderables of the future. A Sino-Russian axis would be a formidable rival to the West, with a combined population of almost 1.3 billion workers, soldiers and consumers, and a sphere of influence stretching from Kaliningrad in the west to Hong Kong in the east.

Ventures such as the PfP, for all their good intentions, only encourage those Russians who see Western delicacy as granting them a free hand to restore their great power status in Eurasia. The irony is, after all, that the PfP's framework document bears a striking resemblance to the founding charter of the CIS, an entity which, if it exists at all, is but a thin and tattered cloak for Russian 'new imperialism'. One does not have to see Boris Yeltsin as another Hitler to fear that the PfP might prove to be another Munich. After all, Russian attitudes over the Conventional Forces in Europe (CFE) Treaty signed in 1990 and the Conference on (later, Organization for) Security and Co-operation in Europe (CSCE/OSCE) already raise grounds for concern.

The CFE Treaty committed the Soviets to withdrawing troops from Central and Eastern Europe and, in many ways, marked the end of the Warsaw Pact. It set limits to the size of forces nations could maintain within Europe (defined as being between the Atlantic and the Urals) and, when the USSR collapsed, the new states generally accepted their share of the Soviet Union's allocation. The one particular problem from Russia's point of view was that CFE granted Ukraine relatively high ceilings as well as the right to

State	MBTs	AFVs	Artillery	Combat Aircraft	Attack Aircraft
Armenia	220	220	285	100	50
Azerbaijan	220	220	215	100	50
Belarus	1800	2600	1615	260	80
Georgia	220	220	285	100	50
Moldova	210	210	250	50	50
Russia	6400	11 480	6415	3450	890
Ukraine	4080	5050	4040	1090	330
Totals	**13 150**	**20 000**	**13 175**	**5150**	**1500**

Figure 9.1: Forces in the former USSR and the CFE Treaty

nationalize much of the most advanced materiel based on its soil. Unrest within and beyond Russia's southern border also led to a desire to strengthen forces on that flank beyond CFE limits. In 1994, for example, the chief of the General Staff, Colonel (now Army) General Kolesnikov, said that Russia's Leningrad and North Caucasus Military Districts together really needed 1100 tanks, 3000 armoured fighting vehicles and 2100 artillery systems. Of these, 600, 2200 and 1000 respectively would need to be based in the Caucasus. Under CFE, though, Russia is actually allowed 700 tanks, 580 armoured fighting vehicles and 1280 artillery systems, as well as 600 tanks, 800 armoured vehicles and 400 artillery pieces in storage.

To an extent, the Russians have a perfectly valid point. CFE was framed in a very different Europe. Then there was no talk of NATO expanding to include former Soviet client states, borders seemed rather more stable than today and, above all, there was still a Union. The war in Chechnya, though, has made the Russians increasingly strident. It has even raised suspicions that they may be planning either openly to flout CFE or try to side-step it by bringing in heavy armour and artillery which was officially part of the Interior Ministry's forces and not the army. Ironically enough, this was a gambit tried by conservatives back in the winter of 1990-91. The invasion also saw Moscow break the terms of the CSCE's Vienna Document on Confidence and Stability Building Measures. This requires disclosure of any concentration of troops over 40 000 strong but no such warning was given. While it is still too soon to draw any firm conclusions, it seemed by 1995 that the interests of Russia and the West were drawing further apart. Instead of building a foreign policy around relations with Washington and the capitals in Europe, Russia seems more prepared to go her own way and even look east for new partners.

THE VIEW EAST: PLAYING THE CHINA CARD?
At the end of June 1994, Chinese Foreign Minister Qian Qichen visited Moscow to set the stage for a summit in September between President Boris Yeltsin and his Chinese counterpart, Jian Zemin. Amidst the usual round of trade deals signed and press conferences held, Qian Qichen found time to address an audience of academics from Moscow State University. Between passages of amiable banality, he made three key points which give some indication of the evolving nature of and strains within Sino-Russian relations: first, that China wants to retain good neighbourly relations 'regardless of how the domestic situation in Russia might change'; second, that China will make no hegemonic claims over Eurasia 'either now or subsequently, when it becomes a great power'; and, third, that China does not yet feel it has achieved anything like its full potential and reforms 'will take another 20 to 30 years' to reach that goal.

It is important to appreciate just how far China is playing a long game at a time when Russia is still lurching from one hurried initiative to another in a desperate struggle for day-to-day survival. As far as Beijing is concerned, it does not matter whether Boris Yeltsin and, indeed, Russian democracy survives, so long as Sino-Russian relations have been uncoupled from domestic politics. China feels that time is on its side. The priority is to defuse Sino-Russian tensions for the medium term; the long term will look after itself. Sino-Russian relations have, after all, a long pedigree of conflict, arguably dating back to medieval Mongol invasion and, most recently, armed clashes along their common border in the mid-1980s.

Their relationship will prove paramount in determining the fate of eastern Eurasia. Qian Qichen went out of his way to distance himself from any suspicions of a more assertive role in post-Soviet Central Asia. He stressed that Chinese relations with the new states were built upon an expectation that their internal links within the framework of the CIS would develop in parallel. To an extent, this was said with an eye to Russian fears. A previous triumphal tour of Central Asia by Chinese Prime Minister Li Peng had seen a new impetus given the campaign to revive the ancient Silk Road route — which linked China with Europe and the Middle East via Central Asia — as a modern trade and communications artery. Accompanied by a phalanx of Chinese businessmen involved in joint ventures and armed with a series of trade concessions, Li Peng forged closer links with the governments of Kyrgyzstan, Turkmenistan and Uzbekistan. He even had some success in calming Kazakhstan, China's most nervous neighbour, although Chinese nuclear tests in 1995 undid much of his good work.

To many in Moscow, this represented a major diplomatic offensive aimed at turning Central Asia eastwards. Zhirinovsky had repeatedly warned of an apocalyptic clash between Russia and China but, this time, more sober voices were also raised in protest. It is worth remembering that the Russian Defence Ministry still routinely revises and updates its plans both to defend against Chinese attack and also to launch a pre-emptive strike. Part of Qian Qichen's agenda was clearly to defuse such worries. A commitment to the existing territorial and political status quo in Asia also reflects underlying domestic worries in Beijing. The Chinese economic miracle has brought with it the threat of the economy over-heating, while also opening the divisions between the centre and the periphery. This is particularly evident in Beijing's unsteady grip upon its northern Xinjiang Uyghur Autonomous Region which abuts nine other countries (Afghanistan, India, Kazakhstan, Kyrgyzstan, Mongolia, Pakistan, Russia, Tajikistan and Tibet). With a population divided between politically dominant Han Chinese migrants, indigenous Uyghurs, as well as Kazakh and Kyrgyz minorities, and containing oil reserves perhaps comparable to those of Saudi Arabia and the Lop Nor nuclear-test site, Xinjiang could prove a test case. In 1990, China deployed 200 000 troops to suppress risings in the west of Xinjiang. Since then, the activities of the Public Security Bureau have been stepped up in response to a campaign of terrorist bombings and repeated reports that weapons were flowing from Afghan and Tajik sources to Islamic Uyghur nationalists. Talk of Uyghur Xinjiang separatism throws into question the whole map of Central Asia. The region's leaders are eager to cultivate Beijing not only as a trade partner but also out of a recognition that most of their nation's boundaries are equally uncertain and disputed.

The reassertive and stable Russia of which Boris Yeltsin dreams is likely to harbour hegemonic ambitions of its own over Eurasia and much of Asia. The experience of Eduard Shevardnadze's Georgia shows that Russian 'aid' can carry with it a hefty political price. On the other hand, were Russia to sink further into economic, social and political disorder, it will hardly be able to do much for its Central Asian allies. Besides, not only may Beijing prove a rather more credible ally but also Russia's very presence in Asia may be at risk if regional separatism continues to develop. Russia's Far East is already a semi-detached partner within the Federation, with a brief historical experience of independence (the Far Eastern Republic of 1918-21) and ethnic, economic and practical ties with China.

Of late, Boris Yeltsin has revived talk of a collective security system for the Asia-Pacific region. What is unclear is what threats this system would be intended to avert. Ideally, it could prove an Asian OSCE, a forum for the solution of regional security problems. Alternatively, it could become the guarantor of a mutually convenient but arguably doomed status quo. This might prove attractive to many leaders but risks locking the member states into attempts to preserve an untenable status quo. That was what happened to the European Alliance system of the late nineteenth and early twentieth centuries, until one relatively trivial problem finally dragged all of Europe into the First World War.

10 Eyes of Russia: the Intelligence and Security Services

Russia's history has often been made by her security services. The original impetus for reforming the USSR came from one of the most able chiefs of its secret police, former chairman of the KGB Yuri Andropov. It was he who groomed Gorbachev and it was Andropov's vassals who first supported *perestroika*. In 1991, the August Coup which brought down the USSR was masterminded by the heads of the security apparatus — and it was the failure of their subordinates to support them which ensured its failure. In 1993, the security forces proved to be Yeltsin's key allies in his battle with parliament and led the way to his October Coup. As for the Chechen debacle of 1994-95, it soon became clear that this was engineered by, and for, the agencies of internal control.

The critical role played by the security apparatus has been reflected in the privileged treatment it has received in the post-Soviet era. For all that he owed his rise to the KGB, Gorbachev had always been ambivalent in his relations with the internal security apparatus. Yeltsin's Russia is marked by no such uncertainty. Indeed, the KGB's successors have become increasingly independent and important. After the 1991 coup, the Russian Ministry of Internal Affairs (MVD) retained control of regular policing, while the KGB was reshuffled rather than reformed. It was broken into separate services, of which the principal five were:

■ the Ministry of Security (MB), established in January 1992, later renamed the Federal Counter-intelligence Service (FSK) and then the Federal Security Service (FSB) in April 1995;
■ the Foreign Intelligence Service (SVR), established in December 1991;
■ the Federal Agency for Government Communications and Information (FAPSI — *Federalnoi agenstvo pravitelstvennoi svyazi i informatsiy*), also established in December 1991;
■ the Main Guard Directorate (GUO — *Glavnoye upravleniye okhrany*), established in December 1991 as well; and,
■ the Federal Border Service (FSG — *Federal'naya sluzhba granitsy*) established in January 1994.

For all the new acronyms, though, the security services changed but little. The KGB's foreign espionage arm, the 1st Chief Directorate, had always been a service within a service. Although it lost a few agents and bases, its re-establishment as the SVR scarcely affected its operations. FAPSI was formed by amalgamating two Soviet institutions, the Government Communications Troops and the KGB's 8th Chief Directorate, which already controlled a sophisticated network of signals intelligence listening stations and code-making and -breaking facilities. The GUO, the president's personal security force, was founded on the basis of the KGB's 9th Directorate, which provided both bodyguards for Soviet leaders and guards for the Kremlin and other key locations. As for the MB, it assumed many of the internal security roles and assets of the KGB. According to government statements, there had been a massive reduction in the size of the staff of the security services, from half a million to 40 000. Yet, almost all of these cuts were accounted for by the establishment of separate organizations for the Border Troops, Government Communications Troops and the like, and the loss of former KGB staff to the new intelligence organizations of the non-Russian republics. As for military intelligence, the operations of the GRU *(Glavnoye razvedyvatelnoye upravleniye)* were scarcely affected.

This round of cosmetic reform became a regular rite. In July 1993, the MB came under the control of Nikolai Golushko. A former career KGB officer who had been responsible for suppressing dissidents in Ukraine, he was hardly a reformist. Golushko had no qualms about supporting Yeltsin against parliament and his decision ensured that the old hands of the KGB who were still in charge of the MB would survive the next reshuffle. On 11 January 1994, Yeltsin issued a presidential decree ratifying the statutes of a new organization, the Federal Counter-intelligence Service (FSK) to replace the MB.

According to this decree, the FSK would be limited to an establishment of 75 000, of whom the central command would account for 1500 officers. On paper, this represented a further and deeper cut in the size of the secret police; yet, once again, the changes were more apparent than real. Press releases spoke of a 46 per cent reduction in the establishment but this figure excluded many security, ancillary and research staff. Component elements of the MB were simply floated off as semi-autonomous agencies. These people were not sacked, merely transferred to other security agencies. These agencies became increasingly numerous. In 1993, for example, the paramilitary Tax Police (NP) and the Presidential Security Service (SBP) — an increasingly powerful off-shoot from the Main Guard Directorate — were established.

This reflects the proliferation of intelligence and security agencies in the

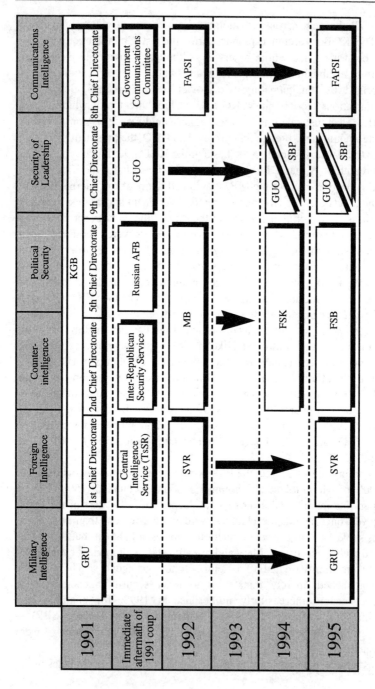

Figure 10.1: The evolution of Russia's intelligence agencies

new Russian government. In January 1994, the government was restructured both to reflect new conditions and to centralize power more tightly into the hands of the president. By mid-1995, this new structure encompasses fully 11 organizations with a security and investigations role. In roughly descending order of importance, they are:

- the Presidential Security Service (SBP);
- the Ministry of Internal Affairs (MVD);
- the Federal Security Service (FSB);
- the Foreign Intelligence Service (SVR);
- the Federal Border Service (FSG);
- the Federal Agency for Government Communications and Information (FAPSI);
- the General Staff's Main Intelligence Directorate (GRU);
- the Main Guard Directorate (GUO);
- the Tax Police (NP);
- the Procurator's Office; and,
- the Military Procurator's Office.

This is a very wide range of services. Some, like the MVD, Procurator's Office and Military Procurator's Office, are first and foremost law-enforcement agencies. The MVD also has sizeable internal security forces, along with the FSG's Border Troops, the SBP and the GUO *(see Chapter 11)*. The NP is a peculiar agency which typifies today's Russia, a hybrid of tax collectors and privatized extortionists. The FSB, FAPSI, SVR and GRU, by contrast, are much more clearly conventional espionage and counter-intelligence services. Tellingly, though, all but the NP share a special subordination to the president. Yeltsin also used the government reform as an opportunity to appoint a new favourite, Yuri Baturin, as his national security aide responsible for liaising between his master and the security services.

THE FEDERAL COUNTER-INTELLIGENCE SERVICE

With Russia's politics in constant turmoil, Boris Yeltsin's main response has been to rely ever more heavily upon the security apparatus. Even before the collapse of the USSR, he had established a specifically Russian KGB. With the dismemberment of the Soviet Union, Russia moved quickly to lay claim to the majority of the KGB's assets, creating its own Federal Security Agency (AFB — *Agenstevo federalnoi bezopasnosti*) in November 1991. Early attempts to create a new type of security service, closer to its Western counterparts, soon came to little. Those reformists and liberals appointed to senior positions were soon ousted, marginalized or domesticated by their former KGB colleagues.

Boris Yeltsin soon proved that he was less interested in cleansing Russian politics of the legacy of the KGB than in establishing a new KGB for his own purposes. In December 1992, he even tried to create a security super-ministry, the Ministry of Security and Internal Affairs (MBVD). This would have brought together the regular police and the political police of the AFB, a concentration of security assets unparalleled since Stalin's time. Of course Yeltsin, whatever his flaws, was, and is, no Stalin, and part of the rationale behind the merger was that the remnants of the KGB could thus be controlled by the MVD. It raised protests from every quarter, from democrats denouncing it as a step towards dictatorship to professional AFB officers resenting their subordination to the MVD. Even the Constitutional Court roused itself to declare the presidential decree void, the first successful challenge to Yeltsin's executive authority. In January 1992, he bowed to the inevitable, reinstating the MVD and establishing the MB.

As already mentioned, this was hardly a blow to the security interests. Security Minister Viktor Barannikov packed the new service with hard-liners, entrusting personnel matters to a man who had actually supported the August Coup in 1991. Although he retained Yeltsin's confidence into 1993, Barannikov had his doubts about the wisdom of an overt move against parliament and thus, in July, he was replaced by Nikolai Golushko. Golushko wholeheartedly supported the October Coup and was then entrusted with creating a new incarnation for the MB following the disastrous showing of pro-presidential candidates in the December elections to the new parliament.

The MB became the Federal Counter-intelligence Service (FSK) in January 1994. The reorganization was presented as a demotion and an opportunity to purge the organization of old-style KGB officers and their ways. In practice, this proved a retrograde step. Although it did lose a few departments and functions, the FSK was almost entirely staffed and headed by formed members of the Soviet police and security apparatus. In February 1994, Golushko was replaced by a former liberal, Sergei Stepashin, but this reflected above all the 'house-training' of Stepashin. Previously a career policeman, Stepashin had become in 1993 deputy security minister and had actually begun calling for more powers to the MB. Perhaps more striking were the appointments at the deputy director level. One, Aleksandr Strelkov, had run Soviet labour camps. Another, Valerii Timofeyev, had been the local KGB chief of the closed city of Gorky (now Nizhnyi Novgorod) and, as such, the jailer of the dissident human rights activist Andrei Sakharov.

More important has been the way that this 'demotion' actually served to bring the FSK more tightly into the president's grasp. As a ministry, the MB did at least have some accountability before cabinet and parliament. The FSK, though, is directly subordinated to the president who also retains the sole right to monitor its activities. Although below establishment, the FSK has quietly assembled a wide range of powers and functions; perhaps, it is fairer to say that the president has.

Presidential Decree 19 of 1994 approved the new statute on the Russian FSK which outlined its role, position and organization. According to this statute, its tasks were six-fold:

■ countering foreign intelligence operations against Russia;
■ gathering information on threats to Russia's security;
■ informing the president of such threats;
■ combating terrorism, drug trafficking and similar criminal threats;
■ protecting Russian state secrets; and,
■ providing counter-intelligence support for the protection of Russia's borders.

In fact, 1994 saw the FSK retain and even expand the MB's empire. The very day it was created, for example, the Russian Security Council considered and approved a report which identified 'economic security' as central to the work of the intelligence agencies. This was defined in extremely broad terms, covering everything from commercial espionage to the penetration and monitoring of areas and organizations whose activities were important to the Russian economy. Taken to its logical conclusion, this would give the SVR the mandate to penetrate the Bundesbank and OPEC, and the FSK the right to investigate any business executive even suspected of links with organized crime. The FSK has taken full advantage of this latitude. It has also retained a section dealing with the political supervision of the armed forces. It was this section which, in the autumn of 1994, recruited serving officers and men for undercover operations in Chechnya without even informing their own commanders. Having already acquired an anti-terrorist commando force, the FSK also established a Special Operations Directorate in September 1994.

By 1995, it had become clear that early hopes that Russia could develop an apolitical democratic security service open to parliamentary scrutiny had come to little. It was responsible only to the president and the handful of liberals within its senior echelons had been purged. In December 1994, Korzhakov's men clashed with the private security guards of a prominent financier with links to the opposition. This led to the dismissal of Moscow's FSK chief, Major General Yevgeni Savostyanov, on the pretext of poor co-ordination with the SBP. He was the last of these liberals and his replacement, Lieutenant General Anatoli Trofimov, left the FSK in the hands of veterans of Soviet-era political policing.

THE FEDERAL SECURITY SERVICE

In April 1995, the FSK became the Federal Security Service (FSB). In part, this was a simple recognition of the fact that the security service had responsibilities far broader than merely countering enemy espionage. It was also a reaffirmation of Yeltsin's determination to create powerful internal security agencies. The Law on the Federal Security Service returns to the FSB most of the assets of the KGB and MB which it had lost in previous reorganizations. These include its Investigations Directorate (with over 1000 officers), 14 remand centres and special armed teams, ranging from personal bodyguards through to trained assassins. It also lifts the last remaining restrictions upon the security apparatus. Now, the FSB can also operate outside Russia's borders, bringing it into direct competition with the SVR. Its agents have the right to enter any property or recruit any informants without permission from the Procurator's Office. In a telling sign of the times, the FSB even has the right to access the new automated balloting systems being introduced in Russia for forthcoming elections, allowing it to record the way each individual casts his or her vote.

The Budyonnovsk incident, where Chechen guerrillas seized much of a southern Russian town, forced the government to open serious talks with the opposition and then negotiated safe passage back to Chechnya, led to another symbolic bloodletting. This had been, after all, a carefully planned large-scale operation and yet the FSB was caught entirely by surprise and could do nothing but watch as the Chechen commander, Shamil Basayev, negotiated with Prime Minister Chernomyrdin. Yeltsin had no real option but to dismiss Sergei Stepashin, even though it raised a difficult question of just who should replace him. After all, from the government's point of view, reforming the FSB took second place to maintaining its loyalties. It had a reputation for marginalizing 'Varangians' as it called outsiders and, thus, all the candidates under discussion would have to come from within the security community. Besides which, there had arisen a serious division between FSB 'insiders' and the burgeoning security empire of Alexander Korzhakov, head of the Presidential Security Service.

In the immediate aftermath of Stepashin's dismissal, his first deputy director, Colonel General Anatolii Safonov, became acting director. A railway engineer by training, he joined the KGB at the age of 24 and spent the next 32 years as a security officer. His main 'internal' rival was Major General Viktor Zorin, the head of the FSB's powerful counter-intelligence directorate and another career security officer. Both would simply continue where Stepashin left off. By contrast, Korzhakov began lobbying Yeltsin to bring the FSB into his orbit. He suggested that the new director should be either his deputy, Georgii Rogozin (who has become infamous as a reputed

Figure 10.2: The Federal Security Service (FSB)

DIRECTOR
Collegium of the FSB
(membership: director, first deputy director,
deputy directors and selected other leading officials)

FUNCTIONAL ORGANIZATIONAL STRUCTURES

Counter-intelligence Operations Directorate

Strategic Facilities' Counter-intelligence Directorate *(remit includes: defence industries, nuclear-power stations, communications centres, dams, space research facilities, etc)*

Military Counter-intelligence Directorate *(monitors: the armed forces, Border Troops, Interior Troops, and other armed formations)*

Economic Counter-intelligence Directorate

Counter-terrorism Directorate

Information and Analysis Directorate

Search Operations Directorate

Investigations Directorate

Special Operations Directorate

Organizational Inspections Directorate

Operational Technical Measures Directorate

Scientific and Technical Support Directorate

Personnel Directorate

Internal Security Directorate

Secretariat

Treaty-Legal Directorate

Registration & Archives Directorate

Public Relations Centre

Logistical Support Directorate

Financial and Economic Directorate

Service Medical Directorate

Service Construction Directorate

Detention Services

TERRITORIAL ORGANIZATIONAL STRUCTURES

Moscow and Moscow Province *(Oblast)* Security Directorate

St Petersburg and Leningrad Province Security Directorate

Territorial Security Offices in each constituent republic, province *(oblast)*, region *(okrug)* and district *(krai)* of the Russian Federation devotee of black magic and parapsychology), or General Mikhail Barsukov, chief of the Main Guard Directorate.

After more than three weeks of behind the scenes wrangling, Barsukov was finally appointed. Not only does this represent a further triumph for Korzhakov, it is also a blow to Prime Minister Chernomyrdin who lobbied against Barsukov's candidature. As is discussed later in this chapter, Korzhakov is no great friend of the prime minister and has staked his political career on Yeltsin's survival. The SPB's Analysis Directorate, which specializes in gathering compromising material, had already begun taking a closer look at Chernomyrdin and, in particular, his links to Gazprom, the privatized gas monopoly within which he used to work. As it is, Korzhakov has assembled an extremely powerful security empire, against which only the army represents a credible counter-weight.

There is always a difference between capability and intent. Boris Yeltsin has shown no desire to use indiscriminate secret police tactics against the Russian people, although his preparedness to unleash them against specific rivals sits uneasily with his declarations of democratic reformism. However, he has presided over a steady recreation of the political police apparatus, driven both by the natural empire building of the secret police themselves and a deeply rooted Russian belief that such forces are necessary to rule such a huge and fractious country. Yeltsin's bequest to the new Russia is a political police force of increasing power, resource and confidence, and whoever succeeds him may be unable or unwilling to resist the temptation to use them more forcefully.

THE FOREIGN INTELLIGENCE SERVICE

Like the MB and FSB, the SVR represents above all a simple evolution of Soviet-era structures. In December 1991, the Russians effectively nationalized the KGB's 1st Chief Directorate, its espionage arm. Yevgeni Primakov, an academician and Middle Eastern specialist with a long-standing relationship with the KGB, was appointed its director general. Many of the existing senior staff, though, remained in place. Like his counterpart at the FSB, the director general of the SVR reports directly to the president.

The 1st Chief Directorate (PGU — *Pervoye glavnoye upravlenie*) had traditionally regarded itself as a cut above the bulk of the KGB, cultivating a reputation as polished and cosmopolitan high achievers. It had also been predominantly ethnically Russian and as such suffered least from the Balkanization of the USSR. Although many officers were soon to leave either willingly or following budget cuts, almost the entire PGU core personnel of 12 000-16 000 was initially transferred to the SVR. Indeed, its organization is almost identical to that of the 1st Chief Directorate and what changes have been made have been done in the name of efficiency, not liberalization. Amidst the economic and political chaos of the post-Soviet order, however, the SVR's operations have not seemed to the government anything near as relevant or necessary as those of the internal security agencies. Between 30 and 40 intelligence networks in the developing world were promptly closed down and the SVR was even forced to reduce its strength in Washington by perhaps a quarter. For its first few years of operation, the SVR seemed unable or unwilling to accept that it could no longer just assume that it had the ear of the government.

It is clear that the SVR mismanaged its relations with the government between 1991 and 1994. The greatest blunder came in 1993 when it tried to involve itself in matters with a direct domestic angle, such as fighting international organized crime. Rightly, the FSK saw this as a bid to muscle onto its turf and launched a furious and effective counter-attack. As a result, the SVR budget and its political status shrank. The initial fragmentation of the USSR cost the SVR some 10 per cent of the assets and personnel of the 1st Chief Directorate and the staff shrank by another 10-20 per cent in the next year or so. Funds once used freely to pay agents have been squeezed steadily, while even officers based at the SVR headquarters at Yasenevo on the outskirts of Moscow are facing problems finding housing.

Despite rumours of his impending transfer, though, Director Primakov began to be given a new prominence in Security Council meetings in 1995. More importantly, he has been promised a more substantial budget share. There are important reasons why the SVR is on the verge of a distinct revival of its fortunes and thus also of its operations in the world.

■ **Economic intelligence.** Instead of concentrating on military espionage, the SVR is looking increasingly at commercial intelligence, ranging from stealing foreign technology to uncovering market-sensitive information to help Russian firms. In 1994, for example, the SVR became alarmed at a proposed deal between Azerbaijan and an international consortium to exploit oil reserves in the Caspian Sea. Primakov decided that this represented a challenge to Russian claims on the Caspian and to her oil revenues. Therefore, he launched a major propaganda campaign, persuaded Yeltsin to threaten sanctions against Azerbaijan and even encouraged the revolt of a local Azeri warlord to bring pressure on the government. Azerbaijan duly signed a 10 per cent stake in the deal over to the Russian firm Lukoil.

■ **Operations in the 'Near Abroad'.** The SVR has managed to develop its own networks within the other post-Soviet states. Although Primakov has repeatedly stated that the SVR does not operate within other CIS states, this has been refuted by the experiences of Russia's neighbours. Given Moscow's interest in regional hegemony and the clear significance of developments within the 'Near Abroad' for Russian political and economic stability, this has further helped the SVR make its case for the relevance of its operations.

■ **Political maturity.** The SVR has also come to terms with its new junior status. Grandiose hopes of challenging the predominance of the FSB and even the SBP have been replaced by a more moderate line. By pointedly refraining from any comment on the FSK's muddled Chechen operation, Primakov finally managed to redeem himself in Stepashin's eyes. More broadly, the SVR has cultivated links with other agencies, collaborating with the NP in investigations of Russian firms abroad and feeding intelligence data more freely than ever to the FSB.

MILITARY INTELLIGENCE

The Chief Intelligence Directorate of the General Staff is a large and highly professional organization, with a proud and strong tradition. It was GRU agents, for example, who uncovered the plans both for the Nazi invasion of Russia in 1941 and the Japanese attack on Pearl Harbour. From the 'Aquarium' or 'Glasshouse', its modern headquarters in Moscow, it deploys global intelligence networks of 'legals' (Russians working abroad on government service such as military attachés) and 'illegals'. It also commands a conventional military intelligence and reconnaissance service with assets ranging from spy satellites to *Spetsnaz* special forces *(see Chapter 13)*. Although the agents of the KGB's PGU used to look down on their military counterparts, calling them *sapogi* (boots), in many ways the GRU has survived the fall of the USSR rather better. While the SVR has been forced to close many of the overseas networks it inherited from the KGB, the GRU has maintained most of its sections in Russian embassies. The GRU and SVR may now have virtually the same number of intelligence officers in the field.

In particular, it retains prime responsibility for four main areas of activity:

■ military and defence-technical intelligence;
■ Central and Eastern Europe — the GRU continues spying on the former Warsaw Pact nations, using the contacts assembled during the years of Soviet domination;
■ CIS 'hot spots' — the GRU monitors developments within the 'Near Abroad', especially where the need for military action may arise; and,

■ spy satellites — through the Military Space Forces, the GRU dominates Russian space-based intelligence.

As with the SVR, though, 1994 saw the GRU shocked out of its complacency. It became clear that it had failed to avoid the corruption so endemic within the armed forces. One journalist was even killed by a bomb while investigating claims that GRU special forces were moonlighting as *mafiya* hit men. Budget crises also took their toll, with salaries often three months in arrears. The GRU was also humbled over the intervention into Chechnya. Both its local station at Vladikavkaz and its central command had repeatedly advised against invasion and GRU *Spetsnaz* had actually been moved out of the region. It later transpired that GRU reports had never even been brought to the attention of the president, blocked by the FSK and SBP.

Consequently, the GRU looked to secure its future and position. The increasing prominence given the chief of the General Staff, Army General Kolesnikov, compared with the defence minister, Army General Grachev, and the new direct link being forged between Kolesnikov and President Yeltsin seems to offer hope. The problem for the GRU is that its chief, Colonel General Fyodor Ladygin, is closer to Grachev than Kolesnikov. Originally appointed in 1992 as a compromise candidate, Ladygin chose to ally himself with the minister, even taking Grachev's son under his wing and sponsoring him for a prestigious GRU commanders' course.

The future looks quite rosy for the GRU, though. Defence Minister Grachev's dismissal looks increasingly likely and when he goes so too will Ladygin. His replacement will probably be appointed by Kolesnikov and thus the GRU will be able to make its peace with the General Staff. What is more, the GRU is finding new friends. One adviser to Prime Minister Chernomyrdin, for example, is Yuri Dulenko, a former deputy chief of the GRU. The GRU's prophetic warnings on Chechnya have also begun circulating belatedly, doing the service no harm at all. Finally, the move towards incorporating Central and Eastern Europe into NATO was not only predicted by the GRU but has also revived interest in specifically military intelligence on the region. One way or another, the GRU is set to become another beneficiary of Russia's evolving attitudes towards the rest of the world.

OTHER AGENCIES: DOES MORE MEAN BETTER?

Not that the above services are Russia's only security and intelligence forces. Russia's desperate budget crisis and, in particular, the problems caused by widespread tax evasion, led in 1993 to the creation of the Tax Police (NP) to police the revenue. From an initial size of 1400, the NP grew to 11 000 by mid-1994, with a target establishment of 40 000 by the end of 1995. Although this may sound relatively innocuous, it is worth stressing that this is not merely a Russian equivalent to the British Inland Revenue or American IRS. It is an armed paramilitary service, staffed largely by former KGB and army officers and with extremely broad powers of search, arrest and self defence. Its director, Lieutenant General Sergei Almazov, had formerly been another KGB chief of Gorky.

The other main agency worth discussing is the Federal Agency for Government Communications and Information (FAPSI). Again, this is essentially part of the old KGB which was split away in December 1991 to form a notionally new body, in this case its 8th (Communications) Chief Directorate along with the KGB Government Communications Troops. Its director since its creation has been Lieutenant General Alexander Starovoitov, formerly deputy chief of the 8th Chief Directorate. Like the US National Security Agency or the UK's GCHQ, FAPSI eavesdrops on foreign radio, telecommunications and other signals traffic and seeks to prevent any such monitoring of Russian communications. To this end, it controls both a central establishment of highly skilled foreign linguists, code-breakers and engineers and a network of listening stations, including a large facility at Lourdes in Cuba.

Unlike Western agencies, however, FAPSI also has an important internal role. With the FSB and SVR, it has been working to help Russian business, not least by hindering the efforts of some Western telecommunications firms to introduce their modern — harder to tap — systems into the country. It has also been struggling to bring all communications media in Russia under its control under the pretext of protecting them against foreign domination. FAPSI's operations are difficult to monitor but cannot be discounted. The 8th Chief Directorate used to consume a quarter of the KGB's entire budget. Unlike many other services, its 85 000 personnel were transferred almost complete to Russian domination, with the loss only of a few listening stations in other republics.

There are also some 6500 private security firms operating within the country. There are two reasons why it is worth noting these private agencies within the context of Russian state intelligence and security forces. First, they reflect the general dilution of the state's monopoly of so many of its basic attributes. The rise of the *mafiya*, the desire by even ministries and banks to have their own security forces, the rising trend towards lynch law in the streets, all represent responses to the state's failure to govern effectively and legitimately. Second, it is often hard to be sure quite where state services end and private agencies begin. The NP, for example, is a state agency but only 20-25 per cent of its operational budget is met by the government. For the rest, it has to rely on a share of any unpaid taxes it can retrieve. FAPSI also runs its own profit-making data and communications services. In addition, there is a large number of senior KGB officers who have set themselves up in business and yet who retain good connections with their former colleagues. For example, Leonid Shebarshin, the former head of the KGB's 1st Chief Directorate, became a security consultant. General Filipp Bobkov, once deputy chairman of the KGB, is now head of corporate security for the powerful *Most* Group, in charge of an estimated 2500 armed security officers and 40 commercial intelligence officers.

This proliferation of agencies raises three wider questions:

■ **Why so many services?** The past four years have seen Russia's security apparatus looking increasingly inward and acquiring an ever wider mandate and range of responsibilities. On one level, these have been an unfortunate by-product of democratization and the shift towards market capitalism. The NP, for example, is a new service whose formation reflects the newly complex economic environment. Similarly, the rise of political terrorism and organized crime has provided new threats to the security and stability of the Russian state. It would, however, be naive not also to see this as a time of empire building and the formation of alliances between the new government and their policemen and secret policemen. Nowadays, almost every ministry wants its own intelligence service, from the Ministry of Finance to the Ministry of Railways.

■ **How well controlled are these services?** There is a dangerous absence of legal and constitutional controls on the intelligence and security agencies. The Duma has been weakened to the point where it cannot exert meaningful oversight, while the president's Security Council is a purely advisory body. Ultimately, they are almost all responsible to the president alone. In practice, though, no one individual can monitor and control such organizations. Instead, control of the security services is purely through the president's personal relationship with, and authority over, them and his ability to play one against the other. In particular, he relies on Korzhakov to keep the rest in order, although whether he does himself or Russia any favours by depending so heavily upon his former bodyguard is another matter. This is a very fragile and unstable state of affairs: personal relations can sour, balances of power can change, and Boris Yeltsin's own physical and political condition is deteriorating steadily.

■ **How useful are they?** It is striking just how unsuccessful this huge array has been. The MB failed either to predict or prevent the rise of the ultra-nationalist Zhirinovsky in 1993-94. The FSK and MVD did little to prevent the criminalization of Chechnya until too late and, when they did launch their clumsy and counter-productive invasion, they did it for their own institutional reasons. General Korzhakov's SBP seems more intent on isolating than informing the president. Intelligence agencies are less than useless if they are unreliable or if their information either fails to reach the decision-makers or is ignored. In February 1995, for example, a series of documents prepared for Gorbachev by the KGB in the spring of 1991 were returned to the FSK, still unopened. They proved to be full of detailed and useful data on the state of the armed forces and the mood of the Soviet republics. Gorbachev's suspicions of the KGB had reached such a pitch, though, that he had not even bothered looking at them. Similarly, the GRU's accurate warnings of the dangers inherent in the invasion of Chechnya never reached Yeltsin's desk, and the intelligence agencies have done much to sour Yeltsin's relations with the West. Former FSK Director Stepashin, for example, had claimed that more spies were uncovered in Russia in 1994 than in any of the past five to seven years. To a large extent, this essentially false claim was a political gambit to prove both his own efficiency and the FSK's need for a greater budget. Yet, it has also contributed to the xenophobic climate of suspicion and betrayal now growing in Moscow.

So the Russian government now deploys an expanding array of security organizations, largely built on the basis of Soviet services and armed with a wide range of powers and responsibilities. Beset with crime, economic crisis and the rising threats of local secessionism and neo-fascism, it is easy to see why Yeltsin wants these powers, but the Soviet era shows the limitations of these organizations. Andropov controlled them but did not really know what he could do with them. Gorbachev tried to use them to reform and found them unprepared to obey him. Yeltsin drew the sword to use against parliament in October 1993. Can he continue to use or sheath it? Either way, is a sword really a useful tool with which to build democracy and prosperity?

11 Hounds of the State: The Security Forces

Cossacks on their shaggy little ponies, sabres and whips in their hands, remain one of the most vivid pictures of the tsarist era, the final defenders of the crown. Like their tsarist predecessors, Soviet leaders relied heavily upon their internal security forces both to keep the masses in line and also limit the danger of a military coup. Lenin was defended by Latvian riflemen, while Stalin spawned whole armies of security troops. Even Gorbachev was prepared to use these 'hounds of the state' in his bid to hold the USSR together. By 1991, there were fully 405 000 internal security troops and paramilitaries, one for every 703 Soviet citizens. To put it another way, the security troops were 10 per cent the size of the regular armed forces.

The Yeltsin era has seen these forces become more, not less powerful. By 1 January 1995, there were 344 000 in Russia, or one for every 436 citizens — almost 20 per cent the size of the regular army. In other words, at a time when the Russian military is struggling to survive, the nation's internal security forces have enjoyed a steady expansion in their size, role and budgets to the point where they are proportionately twice as numerous as in the Soviet era. This reflects both the growing importance of the security forces within Russian politics as well as the evident need for resources to combat the anarchy and criminality which threatens the very survival and effectiveness of the Russian state.

THE MINISTRY OF INTERNAL AFFAIRS

The humiliation of Russia's internal security forces at Budyonnovsk has also further contributed to the militarization of Russia's Ministry of Internal Affairs (MVD). On 30 June 1995, Interior Minister Viktor Yerin was sacked. While loyal to Yeltsin, Yerin's time as minister was an unhappy one for everyone else concerned. Crime rates had continued to rise, the morale of the police had continued to decay and the Interior Troops had become embroiled in a bloody and unpopular war in Chechnya. From the government's point of view, though, his successor would have to tackle three main tasks: first, produce some high-profile (even if largely illusory) successes to convince the

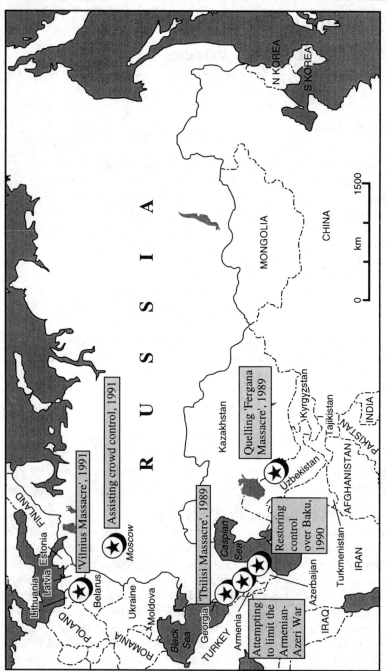

Figure 11.1: Use of the security forces in Gorbachev's USSR

Lithuania
Latvia
Estonia
FINLAND
Vilnius Massacre, 1991
Assisting crowd control, 1991
Moscow
Belarus
POLAND
Ukraine
Moldova
ROMANIA
Black Sea
TURKEY
Georgia
Tbilisi Massacre, 1989
Armenia
Attempting to limit the Armenian-Azeri War
Azerbaijan
IRAQ
IRAN
Caspian Sea
Restoring control over Baku, 1990
Turkmenistan
AFGHANISTAN
PAKISTAN
INDIA
Uzbekistan
Quelling 'Fergana Massacre', 1989
Kyrgyzstan
Tajikistan
Kazakhstan
R U S S I A
MONGOLIA
CHINA
N KOREA
S KOREA
0
km
1500

public of the government's commitment to fighting crime ahead of parliamentary and presidential elections; second, combat the crisis of morale within the police (tellingly, the newly resurgent Communist Party of Russia has reported a dramatic surge in recruitment amongst police officers); and, third, maintain the existing close alliance between the ministry's senior leadership and the present government.

Some advocated a conservative 'business as usual' approach, appointing either of the first deputy interior ministers. One, Colonel General Yevgeni Abramov, had become acting minister on Yerin's dismissal. With a distinguished career record as a detective and no discernible political ambitions, he was a straightforward candidate who would appeal to the police rank and file. The other deputy, Colonel General Mikhail Yegorov, would have been a more political candidate. Unlike Abramov, he had involved himself in politics since the 1980s and has moved to align himself with the new regime. His time as head of the Organized Crime Directorate, though, had not seen particular success, and he had been closely involved with the Budyonnovsk debacle.

To others, especially those still hoping to carry out at least some of the idealistic promises of 1990-91, the answer was to appoint of a civilian, possibly with a background in the Procuracy of the Ministry of Justice. This could have represented a move towards a Western-style separation of policy (the province of elected politicians) and execution (in the hands of professional officials) and been a step towards an equivalent adoption of Western methods of policing. This option was rejected, ostensibly on the grounds that the police would not accept such a candidate. In fact, it was precisely because the regime does not want to abandon the close political control and the emphasis upon public order it inherited from the Soviet regime.

This was proven by the eventual choice of Colonel General Anatoli Kulikov to succeed Yerin. He is neither a policeman nor a politician but a career soldier from the MVD's paramilitary Internal Troops. Born in 1946, at the age of 18 he enrolled in the Ordzhonikidze Higher Internal Troops Military Command School and rose quickly through the ranks. He studied at the General Staff Academy at the same time as Defence Minister Grachev and became overall commander of the Internal Troops in 1992. He was not the only combat general being considered for the post. Another candidate was Colonel General Boris Gromov. Having commanded forces in Afghanistan, Gromov was briefly deputy Soviet interior minister in 1991 when he presided over preparations for a potential declaration of martial law. Eventually, Kulikov was favoured both for his experience commanding the Internal Troops and above all his political reliability. Whereas Gromov is something of a maverick, currently languishing as military adviser to the Foreign Ministry for having criticized the Chechen operation, Kulikov has supported the Yeltsin regime at every turn. He threw his weight behind the suppression of parliament in October 1993 and comes to his new post from Chechnya where he has been in overall command of operations.

His appointment thus reflects the government's determination to maintain close political control over the MVD as well as a determination to yet further militarize it and develop its public order role. While many day-to-day investigations and routine duties are being devolved to local authorities, the focus of the central MVD will increasingly become internal security. This will also be reflected in a redoubling of efforts to update Russia's penal code. In this context, it is worth noting that one officer close to Kulikov has gone so far as to argue — in terms very similar to those favoured by Vladimir Zhirinovsky — that Russia's criminal problem can only be solved by a revival of the Civil War-era 'troikas' of secret police officers empowered to judge and kill suspected criminals on the spot. In his first address as minister, Kulikov sought to allay such fears. 'The ministry needs reforms', he said, 'but no one is going to act drastically'. Nevertheless, an increased emphasis upon policing by force and coercion will inevitably have serious implications for prospects for the democratization of the Russian legal system.

THE INTERIOR TROOPS

The MVD retains the main responsibility for internal security and public order. It controls not only the regular police but also a series of security forces.

■ **Internal Troops**. The MVD's most powerful arm are the Internal Troops (VV). In the Soviet era, there had officially been 350 000 but the overwhelming majority of these were really just prison warders and glorified factory security guards. By mid-1995, most of these secondary functions had been hived off to other organizations. This left a core of trained security troops some 70 000 strong, armed and equipped as light mechanized infantry, with their own tanks, armoured vehicles and helicopters. Just over half are permanently garrisoned in and around main cities, while the 30 000 Operational Designation Forces (*Opnaz — Operativnoe naznacheniya*) are fully mobile. Their trademark brick-red berets and unit badges have become familiar sights in 'hot spots' from Chechnya to the streets of Moscow.

■ **1st Independent Special Designation Division**. The most important *Opnaz* force deserves a special mention. The 1st ODON Division (*1aya Otdeleniya diviziya osobennovo naznacheniya*) is based at Balashikha on

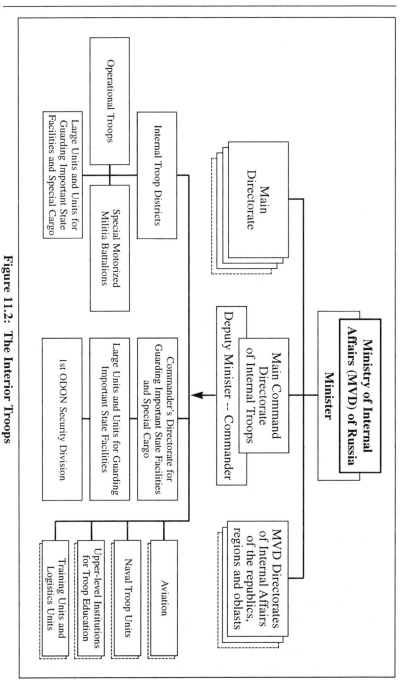

Figure 11.2: The Interior Troops

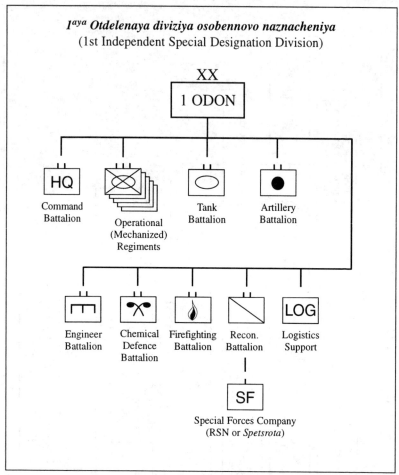

Figure 11.3: 1st ODON

the outskirts of Moscow. It is an oversized mechanized division, some 9000-10 000 strong, with such special additions as a fire-fighting battalion. It was established in 1924 as an elite force to protect Moscow and the Party leadership from counter-revolution. Since 1926, it was known as the Special Designation Independent Motor Rifle Division named after F E Dzerzhinsky, the first head of the Bolshevik secret police. Just as the KGB survived under a new name, so too did Yeltsin decide to save the 'Dzerzhinsky' for himself. After all, the division had an unsullied reputation for obedience to whoever happened to be in the Kremlin. It had supported the August Coup in 1991 and later duly supported Yeltsin's October Coup. In 1994, it was renamed but its role, of counterbalancing the army and other units in the capital, is still the same as it was in 1924. It lost 58 men policing the 'hot spots' until the invasion of Chechnya when it lost another 57 in the first six months of the war alone.

■ **Special Militia Battalions**. The MVD also controls 40 Special Motorized Militia Battalions (SMBM — *Spetsial'nyi motorizovannyi batal'on militsii*), each around 1000 strong and based in major Russian cities. These are similar to the garrison VV forces but less heavily armed. Their main roles are two-fold. First, they support and reinforce the city's regular police which can involve anything from crowd control at football matches to supplying armoured cars in which to raid *mafiya* hideouts. Second, they also patrol the city's rural hinterland, fighting the rising tide of banditry in the countryside. Several were also deployed in Chechnya, albeit they rarely distinguished themselves. It may be harsh but fair to say that they are a haven for recruits who could not reach the standards of the *Opnaz* and who lacked the motivation to become regular police officers.

■ **Special Forces**. In the past, the MVD also controlled a variety of special counter-terrorist and special operations forces. Some have since been transferred to other agencies, while others are instead subordinated to local police commands. There is an elite force, the Special Designation Company, within the 1st ODON. In theory, the MVD also controls the *Vympel* anti-terrorist group. Originally established as part of a trio of KGB special forces in 1974, it has almost ceased to exist. Most of its officers resigned or retired in response to their transfer from the (now defunct) Security Ministry to the MVD. They resented the way the decision was made without consultation as well as the lower salaries and prestige of the MVD. *Vympel* may be reconstituted as a force tasked with dealing with the threat of nuclear terrorism but, as of writing, there has been no progress in resuscitating the unit.

POLICE AND PARAMILITARIES

In the Soviet era, the distinction between the police and army was always rather blurred. The police — called the militia — were armed, wore uniforms much like army officers and even bore military ranks. Russia's police today are going even further down this route, undergoing a rapid process of paramilitarization. While still under-paid and over-stretched, police officers are increasingly being issued with body armour and assault weapons. After all, as crime becomes increasingly violent, the borderline between law enforcement and combat duty is becoming ever more blurred. Almost 200 died or went missing in 1994 alone. It is already commonplace to see even the traffic police (GAI — *Gosudarstvennaya avtomobil'naya inspektsiya*) patrolling with sub-machine guns and tear gas sprays, while most towns and cities now boast one or more assault units with a range of weapons and munitions to make any Russian soldier jealous.

■ **Police commandos**. Like the VV, the Russian police contain several specialized commando forces, the Specialized Designation Militia Detachments (OMSN — *Otryad militsii spetsial'novo naznacheniya*). The first such anti-terrorist unit was established in 1977 during the preparations for the Moscow Olympics in 1980. OMSN units exist in Moscow, St Petersburg and some other major cities and vary wildly in their professionalism and expertise. The Moscow OMSN is subordinated to the city police Criminal Investigations Directorate (MUR — *Moskovskii ugolovnyi rozysk*), and has become primarily a *mafiya*-busting force.

■ **Special Designation Militia Detachments**. The rising crime and violent unrest of the late Soviet era led in 1987 to the creation of the Special Designation Militia Detachments (OMON). These paramilitary riot police became a hybrid of police SWAT (special weapons and tactics) forces. They were distinctive for their black berets, grey overalls and long flexible rubber truncheons ironically nicknamed '*perestroika* sticks'. OMON, for example, were used to suppress nationalists in the Baltic states, Transcaucasia and Ukraine. Most of the new states have retained their OMON. In Russia, OMON are based in 49 cities, ranging in size from a usual strength of 100-300 to 1400 in Moscow; the capital has two units, one for the city and one for the region. Overall, there are around 10 000 such police in Russia, some units now titled Special Rapid Reaction Detachments (SOBR — *Spetsial'nyi otdel bystrovo reagirovaniya*). They have also kept up their role as the Kremlin's enforcers: 'black berets' were used to suppress parliament in October 1993 and also in the invasion of Chechnya in 1994-95.

■ **Rapid Reaction Group**. Whereas OMON are subordinated to regional police commands, individual precincts have established their own type of special police unit called the Rapid Reaction Group (GNR). These are much closer to US SWAT or British Armed Response Teams in concept, often just a handful of officers with extra firearms training. To a large extent, they are purely law-enforcement resources, except that in some major cities (notably Moscow, St Petersburg and Yekaterinburg) there are enough of them that they can be brought together in an emergency to provide additional paramilitary forces. This is especially true of Moscow. There, the creation of a Public Security

Militia (*Militsiya obshchestvennoi bezopasnosti*, creating the unfortunate acronym MOB), responsible to the mayor's office as well as neighbourhood Municipal Militias, has led to a proliferation of paramilitaries. Across the whole country, there are perhaps 8000 of these special police.

THE BORDER TROOPS

Reflecting both its long and exposed borders and its habitual paranoia, the USSR built up its Border Troops (PV — *Pogranichnye voiska*) until they almost represented yet another army at the Kremlin's disposal. At its peak, the PV amounted to just under a quarter of a million men, with its own air and naval wings and an arsenal of weapons up to light tanks and artillery. Understandably, this was more than just a glorified customs service: the PV had a proud tradition as the first guardians of the Soviet border. Border Troops were the first to meet the Nazi onslaught in 1941 and clashed with Chinese troops in 1968-69.

The PV were subordinated to the KGB and, following the collapse of the USSR, they were transferred to a new Commonwealth Committee for the Protection of the State Border (KOGG — *Komitet po okhrane gosudarstvennoi granitsy*). Moscow soon asserted its control over the majority, establishing its own Border Troops of the Russian Federation (PVRF). On paper, there are almost 250 000 Russian Border Troops. In practice, the PVRF is around 25 per cent under-strength, leaving the 190 000 'green caps' an unenviable task. They must control 58 000 km of border, stretching from icy Siberian coast to the mountains of the Caucasus. They are also being deployed in other states of the 'Near Abroad' to help protect Russian border interests, as 'neighbourly assistance' and as a show of strength. Some 15 000 serve in Turkmenistan, 2500 in Kyrgyzstan and perhaps another 2000 in Georgia and Armenia. The main deployment is in Tajikistan where Russian Border Troops make up the majority of the 25 000-strong force supporting a pro-Moscow regime against Afghan-backed rebels. The PVRF have also seen action in Chechnya where they have been used to prevent weapons from being smuggled in to the rebels.

Its new role in protecting Russia's interests in the 'Near Abroad' has given the PVRF a new role and standing. Since December 1993, it has been an independent service and its commander, Colonel General Andrei Nikolayev, has been brought onto the President's Security Council. Although a former regular army officer, Nikolayev has thrown himself into the development of the PVRF. He fought off the Defence Ministry's bid to swallow up the Border Troops so successfully that he might even prove a candidate to replace Defence Minister Grachev in due course.

THE PRAETORIANS

As already noted, Boris Yeltsin has built up a powerful array of security forces responsible only to him. Most have been brought under the control of the Main Guard Directorate (GUO) or its increasingly dominant off-shoot, the Presidential Security Service (SBP):

■ **Main Guard Directorate of the Russian Federation.** The GUO is responsible for maintaining public order and political security in Moscow. Its charges including such key sites as nuclear-power stations and the APN Building which also houses Moscow's inter-bank currency exchange. Its 15 000 troops and bodyguards include a commando team and selected elements transferred from the military, reportedly including the 118th Airborne Regiment and the 27th Motorized Brigade.

■ **Presidential Security Service.** The SBP was established in December 1993 out of the GUO. Originally simply formed on the basis of Yeltsin's bodyguards, it grew steadily in both size and powers. Its commander, Major General Alexander Korzhakov, has emerged as one of modern Russia's kingmakers. He has certainly come a long way from his time as Yeltsin's watchman and tennis partner. Its establishment strength is now around 10 000, including the 5500-strong Presidential Guard Regiment (formerly the Kremlin Guard), specialized bodyguards and an elite anti-terrorist commando force.

In theory, the GUO is the senior service. In practice, the SBP is far more powerful given Korzhakov's success at marginalizing or incorporating those agencies rivalling it for control of Moscow. Lieutenant General Mikhail Barsukov, originally head of the GUO, was not only related to Korzhakov by marriage but he had become reconciled to Korzhakov's higher political profile. In effect, he took orders from Korzhakov and then went on to become director of the Federal Security Service (FSB), still at the behest of his notional subordinate. The other challengers to Korzhakov's security pre-eminence in Moscow have also been undermined. The Moscow Directorate of the Federal Counter-intelligence Service (FSK) represented the most serious threat to the SBP's monopoly, something encouraged by Yevgenii Savostyanov, its first director. One of the handful of genuine liberals remaining within the FSK (now the FSB), Savostyanov fought to maintain some notion of 'checks and balances' within the new Russia and thus came to fear and resist the SBP's predominance. Already out of favour with FSK Director Sergei Stepashin, Savostyanov was sacked in December 1994 thanks in part to a provocation organized by the SBP when it raided the motorcade of a senior banker. Savostyanov's fall not only consolidated the grip of former KGB professionals on the FSK but also opened a window for Korzhakov to reaffirm his grip on the capital. As for Moscow's police command, its Main Internal Affairs Directorate, this has no real political role left.

Korzhakov is not just a secret policeman, though. He is also a powerful political actor with his own agenda. He has great influence over Yeltsin and, in particular, is able largely to control what intelligence reports ever get to the president. Aware of his patron's unsteady grip on power, he is clearly also laying the foundations for a potential emergency regime. From the first, the SBP acquired the martial law plans which were established under the Brezhnev era under the codename *Metel* (Blizzard); they have been steadily updated ever since. Many of the recent changes within the SBP and the security apparatus as a whole can be interpreted in terms of *Metel*. Even though such an operation may still appear unlikely, Korzhakov is determined to be ready should the need arise. This combination of personal empire-building and the preparations for possible emergency rule are behind current attempts to expand the size and scope of the SBP's paramilitary arm. In 1995, Korzhakov floated the notion that Russia needs a National Guard.

The idea of a Russian National Guard is not new. In 1990-91, it was used by Boris Yeltsin and his erstwhile deputy Alexander Rutskoi as a means to create a Russian army separate from the Soviet structure. Since the collapse of the USSR, the idea has surfaced periodically in military debate. What is distinctive about Korzhakov's notion is its inherent political role. This National Guard would be an avowedly Praetorian force, in Korzhakov's words 'an instrument in the struggle for political power'. It would be responsible to the president and scattered throughout the country so that it would not only maintain order but also be the president's eyes, ears and if necessary fists in the provinces. As the Caesars knew, though, the swords of the Praetorian Guard had two edges; they could save an emperor, but could as easily topple one.

THE FUTURE: WHO GUARDS THE GUARDIANS?

Today, Russia thus disposes of almost 350 000 largely professional security troops at a time when the regular armed forces are in decline and increasingly staffed by unwilling and substandard conscripts. Yet, what is their role? There is certainly no lack of threats to the internal security and stability of the Russian Federation, extending from inter-ethnic and inter-communal violence to organized crime and *bunt* (that characteristically Russian explosion of mob violence). The paradox is that the size of the internal security forces has not led to commensurate success. One reason for this is to be found in the political struggles taking place between agencies eager to

---

Figure 11.4: Russia's security armies

Anti-Terrorist Commando Forces

Various	c 1000

Militarized Security Forces

Internal Troops (VV)	70 000
Border Troops (PV)	190 000
Presidential forces (GUO/SBP)	25 000

Paramilitary Police Forces

OMON	10 000
Special Motorized Militia Battalions	40 000
Other	8000

Total:	**344 000**

---

stake out their claims to roles and thus funding. Not only are various forces thus competing with each other but they are also facing challenges from other agencies such as the newly resurgent Cossack vigilantes, private security firms and the army.

This largely reflects the wider problem facing Russia's internal security forces, their lack of a clear doctrine and sense of purpose. Are they first and foremost guardians of the constitutional order or presidential praetorians? Should they be controlled on a local level and thus responsible to the community or through central structures? Are they security troops or police officers? Until these questions are resolved, then whatever the size of the internal security budget and however many such agencies are created, Russia's slide into crime, anarchy and disorder looks set to continue.

12 The New Russian Army

By 1 January 1995, the Russian armed forces officially numbered 1 905 000. While still larger than the USA's, it is difficult to decide whether they are a powerful force or a hollow farce. The simple seizure of Groznyy from a rag-tag band of mercenaries, gunmen and volunteers took this army over a fortnight and had to be done by a force cobbled together of odd regiments from here and battalions from there. Paradoxically, the answer is that the Russian armed forces are both. They are under-manned, riven by internal dissent and discontented. Nevertheless, their nuclear arsenal is capable of wiping out all life on the planet several times over. They maintain a core of operational troops and advanced military hardware. There is also a huge potential mobilization base of reservists who have done their time as national servicemen, about 20 million in total. These all ensure that, if the day comes when the Motherland truly is in danger or a leader or regime is able to revive the Russian state, then this will be a formidable military machine.

PAVEL GRACHEV AND THE RUSSIAN DEFENCE MINISTRY
Boris Yeltsin appointed Pavel Grachev as Russia's first defence minister in May 1992. It was an appointment driven more by politics than military logic. After a 'good war' in Afghanistan, Grachev commanded the airborne forces. As such, he had been one of the generals whose refusal to support the 1991 August Coup ensured its failure. To Boris Yeltsin, he was a useful choice. He was young, enthusiastic and popular with his men. Above all, he was loyal and enough of an outsider to the Defence Ministry (traditionally dominated by the Ground Forces) that he would not represent any sort of a political challenge.

Grachev has certainly been no threat to Yeltsin and, despite his own misgivings, has supported the president at every crisis, whether shelling parliament in 1993 or invading Chechnya in 1994. He has, however, been a disastrous defence minister. A 'fighting general', he has manifestly failed to master the bureaucratic and political realities of his job. Instead, he has retreated into the company of a handful of friends and cronies who probably feed him an over-rosy view of the ministry's plight. He even suggested that Groznyy could be captured within a week by a single airborne regiment. He failed to win the armed forces the budget it needs: in 1994, for example, they received less than half the sum they were officially promised. He has failed to provide leadership and inspiration to a military unsure of its place and role, while his reform programmes have largely proved unrealistic or inappropriate.

The result is a military establishment in a state of chaos and despair. Although the official strength at the beginning of 1995 was nearly two million, this was actually probably closer to 1.3 million. Many units are at only half strength and officers are having to carry out even the most menial of duties, from mounting guard to cooking breakfast. At the time of writing, perhaps the only factor keeping Grachev in office is the lack of an obvious and uncontroversial successor on whom both Yeltsin and the military could agree. Most discussion has centred upon five possible candidates:

■ **Army General Mikhail Kolesnikov**, chief of the General Staff. Ironically enough, the main resistance to the appointment of this able and effective commander would come from Kolesnikov himself. He has established a relatively comfortable niche for himself and, as the role of the General Staff expands, would seem to have little inclination to move to the more politically exposed post of minister.

■ **Colonel General Boris Gromov.** Until the invasion of Chechnya, Gromov looked a strong candidate. A Hero of the Soviet Union from his days as a commander of forces in Afghanistan, he is popular with troops and public alike, with a reputation for successfully combining the roles of soldier and administrator. He has never been a favourite of Yeltsin's, though. In 1990, he stood for election to the Russian vice-presidency in opposition to Yeltsin's ticket and his involvement in the 1991 August Coup remains unclear. He was for a while close to Vice-President Rutskoi. Gromov has never felt the need to hide his views. His open criticisms of the Chechen intervention saw him effectively sacked from his job as a deputy defence minister and shunted into a rather less significant job as military adviser in the Foreign Ministry. It is unwise, though, ever to assume that Gromov is out of the race.

■ **Colonel General Andrei Nikolayev**, commander of Border Troops. Nikolayev is certainly a man to watch. Following his successful fight in 1994 to resist the incorporation of his command into the army, he won his political spurs. More importantly, this brought him to Boris Yeltsin's attention and he has clearly become a presidential favourite, as was Grachev in his time. Finally, he has shown himself to be an able administrator, with the diplomacy required by the fact that many of his troops are based in neighbouring countries. Whether he has the allies and the experience to become defence minister, though, is another matter. What is not clear is whether the Ground Forces' clique dominating the ministry would resent him for his time in the Border Troops or accept him given that previously he was an army man. Nor did he come well out of the Budyonnovsk hostage crisis discussed in Chapter 7. Although he tried to argue that the Border Troops' job was to seal Chechnya's outer borders rather than those with Russia, he was not helped by the fact that the Chechen guerrillas made their daring attack on the very day the Border Troops issued a statement congratulating themselves on the new security measures they had established all around the war zone. Whereas the interior minister and Federal Security Service director were sacked in the aftermath of the incident, Nikolayev merely suffered embarrassment. Nevertheless, it forced him to adopt a rather low profile for a while.

■ **Andrei Kokoshin**, first deputy defence minister. The absence of uniformed candidates might reflect an opportunity for Yeltsin to grasp a long-standing nettle and appoint an outsider. As the only civilian to have been appointed a defence portfolio and an expert on disarmament issues, Kokoshin might represent a suitable compromise. At first, he faced resistance and isolation within the ministry. Since then, though, he has been able to consolidate his position, with the creation of two parallel chains of command, Kolesnikov handling operations and Kokoshin dealing with support and supply.

■ **Lieutenant General Alexander Lebed**. A real outsider would be the outspoken Lebed who, in 1995, announced his retirement. He has a high profile and a strong constituency within the army and country but neither Yeltsin nor the ministry would be happy to see him appointed. The High Command sees him as erratic and unpolitic, poorly suited to the needs of the post. There is lobbying for Lebed in Moscow but, as his eyes may be upon the presidency, a term managing decline in the Defence Ministry and being raked over the coals in parliament may undo the careful cultivation of his blunt 'fighting general' image.

Perhaps the real answer is that it matters far less just who succeeds Grachev. As mentioned above, the role of General Kolesnikov and his General Staff has grown steadily. It has become directly responsible to the president instead of the defence minister, something confirmed in the new Law on Defence. The chief of the General Staff now sits on the important Security Council in his own right. Indicatively, Kolesnikov was promoted to the rank of army general in 1995. The ministry is increasingly concerned with the nuts and bolts of running an army, while the General Staff controls operational matters and formulates strategy. This reflects a general strengthening of the president's personal control over the military. After all, the Laws on Defence and Peacekeeping (1995) give him the right to declare martial law and suspend the constitution at will, define military doctrine and even launch nuclear first strikes at his own discretion.

What this means is that not only is the identity of the new minister less important but also the demands of the job are changing. After Shaposhnikov and Grachev, two able officers but light-weight ministers, the armed forces cannot risk a third. Nevertheless, the minister's job is increasingly that of administrator, political figurehead and representative. A civilian might be able to do a better job in playing Russian politics, without raising fears of coups. Whoever is in charge, though, will have urgently to address the problem of reforming the Russian military.

MILITARY REFORM: RENOVATION OR DISINTEGRATION?

Once it became clear that the CIS would never represent a viable (and Russian-dominated) military structure, a Russian Defence Ministry was established in April 1992. Ironically enough, Grachev drew upon a reform programme designed by the old Soviet defence minister as his own broad blueprint for change. Reform of the Russian military would take place in three phases:

■ **1992-93**. The first phase would be a stock-taking, as the new Russian Defence Ministry inventoried its new forces and arranged the withdrawal of forces on foreign soil.

■ **1993-95**. The second phase would be a reform of the overall command structure, creating new rapid-deployment Mobile Forces (MS — *Mobilnye sily*) and shifting the balance of recruitment from conscription to volunteer service *(see Chapter 13)*. The end of 1993 also saw the introduction of a new military doctrine, the theoretical basis on which all further plans would be based *(see Chapter 3)*. Amongst its innovations, it makes the army responsible for the protection of Russians in the 'Near Abroad'.

■ **1995-2000**. The third phase would be a reorganization of the field forces to create smaller but more flexible formations based on brigades and corps instead of the old divisions and armies. The command structure would also be reformed. The existing five branches of service (army, air force, navy, air defence, strategic deterrence) would become three: army, navy and air force, incorporating both air defence and nuclear forces.

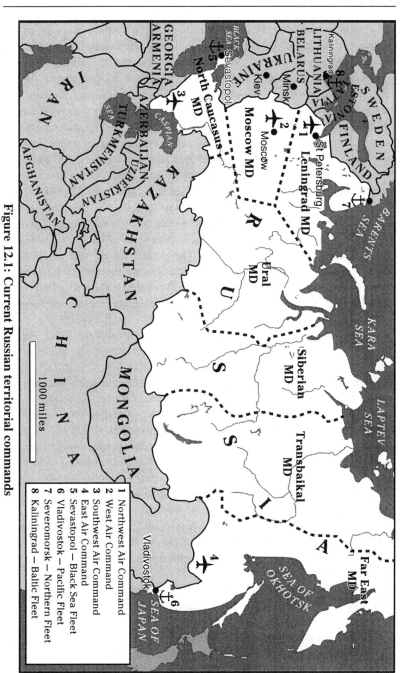

Figure 12.1: Current Russian territorial commands

1 Northwest Air Command
2 West Air Command
3 Southwest Air Command
4 East Air Command
5 Sevastopol — Black Sea Fleet
6 Vladivostok — Pacific Fleet
7 Severomorsk — Northern Fleet
8 Kaliningrad — Baltic Fleet

On paper, this was all very well, but the ministry lacked above all the budget to take many of these steps. Grachev characterized the 1994-95 defence budget as 'ruinous' and 'criminal', warning of a collapse in the morale, combat readiness and mobilization base of the armed forces. Currently, the plans are foundering on a lack of resources. Procurement stands at only a quarter of the level which the ministry and military-industrial complex would like. Some 180 000 officers have no accommodation. Unable to pay competitive salaries, the armed forces simply cannot recruit enough volunteers. Perhaps the only 'real' reforms taking place are those which go with rather than against the grain of developments in Russia, moving towards rationalization and decentralization. Reorganization of functional and territorial commands should go some way to reducing the inter-service rivalries currently bedeviling the armed forces. At the moment, for instance, all five branches fly aircraft. It should also clear the way for some pruning of the top-heavy military bureaucracy. The armed forces will be divided between central forces — largely strategic assets and the new Mobile Forces — and integrated territorial commands. The latter has been trailed, with mixed results, in the Far East and Kaliningrad, under Lieutenant General Viktor Chechevatov and Admiral Yegorov respectively. Eventually, there will be four such joint territorial commands; North (to include the Baltic Fleet); South (the North Caucasus); the Far East; and a reserve and training command, the Urals-Transbaikal. Although running behind schedule, these are to become operational by the end of 1995 or mid-1996, leaving the central region directly commanded from Moscow. Each command is to be headed by a figure with rank equivalent to a deputy defence minister. This reflects not only their importance but also the extent to which they will be allowed — indeed, encouraged — to operate autonomously during peacetime. After all, Russian politics and the Russian economy have been broken into local polities. Furthermore, with central budgets over-stretched, units have had to come to terms with this and build themselves roles within regional systems. Commanders will be both Moscow's local proconsuls, there to maintain the authority of the centre, and regional wheeler-dealers, working to keep their troops fed and disciplined. If anything will, it is such triumphs of pragmatism over abstract military theory that will keep the Russian army alive and united.

As for the individual arms of service, except for special and intervention forces, they are in various degrees of disrepair:

■ **The Strategic Forces.** While engaged in dismantling weapons in accordance with START I, Russia is still committed to maintaining a global nuclear reach. By the end of 1994, Russia deployed 773 intercontinental ballistic missiles (ICBMs), another 728 submarine-launched ballistic missiles and 1596 strategic bombers. The older missiles are being withdrawn to meet START targets, while new systems are also being deployed, including the new silo-based Topol-M ICBM (SS-25), first launched in December 1994. Russia has suggested it will maintain forces at the maximum levels permitted by the START treaty and even increase them to the higher levels permitted under the terms of START II. The more advanced missiles currently in place will mainly have exhausted their serviceability by the year 2000, however, while regular tests are needed to maintain operational effectiveness.

■ **The Ground Forces.** The army is facing a crisis of equipment and personnel. It is at only half the established strength, the number of operational and near-operational divisions falling from 48 in 1994 to 22 in 1995. In the past two years, the Ground Forces received only 22 per cent of the new weapons and equipment they needed.

■ **The Air and Air Defence Forces.** Until the promised reforms are enacted, Russia effectively retains four air forces: Strategic Aviation, Air Defence Forces, Frontal Aviation and Transport Aviation. Budget cuts have hit them all, slashing procurement levels and reducing training by over half. Air force commander Lieutenant General Pyotr Deinekin has noted that while the air forces were scheduled to shrink by a third between May 1992 and the end of 1995, little of the remainder would be genuinely airworthy in the absence of modern training facilities.

■ **The Navy.** While only funded at 47 per cent of the level promised, elements of the navy are relatively combat ready, especially its Northern Fleet. Nevertheless, ships are poorly maintained, supplies and sailors lacking and combat training run on a shoestring. The navy's problems also risk affecting the rest of the country. It owes the civilian economy 105 billion roubles in unpayable debts. There are also 78 decommissioned nuclear submarines whose nuclear fuel the navy claims to be unable to remove and make safe.

THE RUSSIAN SOLDIER

Glasnost' brought to light many social and disciplinary problems within the Soviet armed forces. Bullying, drug abuse, alcoholism, ethnic friction and corruption, all were discussed with unprecedented candour. However, it was not just that existing problems were being increasingly freely covered, they steadily worsened through the 1980s. Just as the political authorities found themselves at once unable to apply old methods of control and a long way from developing new ones, the military authorities were presented with a challenge they could not meet. It stemmed from a variety of causes.

Society, especially the culture of the young male cohort, had changed markedly since the Stalinist times when the Soviet 'military feudal' pattern was instituted. Central to that pattern was a concept of the soldier as uneducated but disciplined, rote trained with a few basic skills and prepared to act with blind obedience to orders from high. Yet, Soviet youth became increasingly educated and sophisticated, acquiring the leisure time and freedom from all-embracing political control to develop its own cultures and attitudes. In effect, there was a re-emergence of classes in society since Stalin. Middle-class young men, relatively wealthy and cosmopolitan, increasingly monopolized university education and evaded military service. Working-class children, still more technically oriented and sophisticated than their parents and grandparents, had been alienated by a state which locked them out of the elite. The result was a conscript far more skilled and flexible than his 1940s' counterpart but less prepared to put up with hardship, strict discipline and monotony to defend his country from a threat he was unlikely either to believe or to fear. At a time when Soviet manpower planners were already worried about what they unofficially called the 'yellowing' of the army as a result of the far greater birth rates of the USSR's Central Asia and Transcaucasian populations, Slav recruits proved increasingly prone to draft-dodging.

Nor could the authorities simply try to restore old ways at a time when the official line was of reform and progress. Democratization and nationalism brought to an end the neat and comforting certainties of the past. A crisis in the confidence of the Young Communist League relaxed even Party discipline in the ranks. Along with greater candour about the problems of the USSR, this undermined the potent mix of Soviet nationalism and Party dogma, historically the bedrock of Soviet military discipline. The new generation's role models were not the clean-limbed proletarians of official myth but rock stars, pacifist balladeers and street-wise non-conformists.

In many ways, the real problem facing the armed forces was that they did not want to return to all the old ways. Afghanistan brought home the inadequacies of 'military feudalism'. Modern weapons need skilled technicians, not loyal cannon-fodder. Small unit tactics were becoming increasingly important and hence the initiative of conscript non-commissioned officers and junior officers an asset to be nurtured. The Soviets eventually admitted that it took the average draftee at least a year to become an effective soldier. Given that soldiers generally served for two years, and that the last few months were generally overtaken by the countdown to demobilization, this meant that each draftee was only combat ready for 6-8 months! Since then, though, the human problems facing the Russian military have only grown:

■ **Under-manning**. The national service system has largely collapsed; conscripts do not want to serve, and the local police have better things to do than try to enforce the draft. Those who are drafted are generally the least educated or see it as an alternative to prison — some 20 per cent of those accepting call-up have already committed a criminal offence.

■ **Disorder**. In part as a result, crime, drug abuse and bullying within the ranks are endemic. Four out of every five conscripts will at some point be beaten. For one in three, this will be so severe that they are hospitalized. One in 20 will be the victim of homosexual rape.

■ **Poverty**. Professional soldiers, largely officers, have seen their salaries devoured by inflation; six-monthly pay rises have never kept pace with the rocketing price of living. By 1994, a major general was being paid a third as much as a factory worker.

■ **Homelessness**. Units are squeezed into crumbling barracks, especially those withdrawn from Central and Eastern Europe or former Soviet republics. As for the officer corps, around one in four has no accommodation for himself and his family. Thousands are having to live in the cheapest slums or even unheated tank sheds and tents.

■ **Ill-health**. Overcrowding, poor diets and a lack of spending on medical care have all contributed to a serious health problem within the military. One in five conscripts leaves the army chronically ill.

■ **Disorientation**. Once the Soviet soldier was a much-feted 'defender of the motherland'. Most conscripts at worst accepted their lot as a necessary duty; at best, they saw it as a chance to earn new skills and gain manhood. The officer corps was privileged and highly regarded. Above all, officers and men alike knew their role in society, their historical traditions and the contours and ideals of the state they were defending. Today, soldiers are vilified, paid a pittance and do not even have the resources to fulfil their mission. Nor are they even sure what that mission is: are they merely defenders of the new Russia or do they have a wider responsibility in the 'Near Abroad'? Are they Yeltsin's praetorians or apolitical servants of the people? Are they combat troops or glorified riot police?

It is thus not surprising that young Russians are dodging the draft, that dedicated and able officers are leaving in their droves and that soldiers are turning to crime *(see Chapter 6)* or extremist politics. In the parliamentary elections of December 1993, for example, perhaps a third supported the neo-fascist Vladimir Zhirinovsky. Many others express an open admiration for Alexander Lebed in his criticisms of Yeltsin and Grachev. This should not be taken as meaning that the army is full of fascists. Officers who praise Lebed also admit that he would probably be a terrible president or defence minister. Equally, few would want to find themselves involved in the new round of wars of expansion which Zhirinovsky talks of starting. Instead, these are protest votes, one of the few ways that Russian soldiers have of expressing their deep resentment at their plight.

DREAMS AND REALITIES

On paper, Russia still intends to maintain a flexible and formidable military machine. It will have a sizeable, high-technology, high-mobility core force able to deploy to meet threats from any direction and fight both a war of offence or a defence in depth. Russia's reach will be global, from her nuclear missiles to her ocean-going navy. Yet, Russia cannot afford such military forces and postures. The 1995 Federal Budget Law envisages spending 48.6 trillion roubles on national defence, some 20 per cent of the total. To this, though, should be added various defence-related expenditure, including maintaining the Interior Army (1.4 trillion) and Border Troops (2.3 trillion), subsidies to support regions devoted to defence research (1 trillion), support for mobilization training and civil defence (1 trillion), and unquantifiable amounts supporting defence production and the military-related activities of the Ministry of Railways as well as the Ministry of Civil Defence, Emergencies and Natural Disasters. These bring the total figure to over 54.3 trillion roubles, 22 per cent of the whole budget.

Even so, this is not even enough to maintain existing force levels, for which the defence minister had demanded 44 per cent of the entire budget. However, Russia does not need such forces. The real threat comes not from NATO or the Chinese but instability on Russia's borders and, above all, unrest at home produced by the economic crisis. In reality, the government wants to maintain forces as able to intervene at home as within the 'Near Abroad'. It also hopes to avert the danger of the army becoming a political threat by reasserting its personal relationship with the head of state and paying lip service to its concerns.

This cannot go on for long, though. The attempt to maintain a superpower military machine on a developing world budget is ruinous. Soon Russia must either devote more resources to the military or seek instead to create credible forces within existing budgetary limitations. Either has serious political costs but without any such decision being made, though, the Russian armed forces will continue to decay into uselessness at best, warlordism at worst.

13 Russia's Long Arm: Special and Intervention Forces

The former Soviet military machine was perhaps best known for its size, for its division after division of goose-stepping conscript infantry. Yet, its spearhead forces had always been a relatively distinct array of elite and intervention units. It was, for example, commandos and paratroopers who seized Budapest in 1956 and Prague in 1968. They were the first into Afghanistan in 1979 and the last out in 1989. When the Azeri capital Baku rose in effective rebellion in 1990, it was again the paratroopers who brought it back into the Soviet fold. It was the decisions of paratroop commanders to defy the 1991 August Coup that finally ensured its collapse. They were a distinct cut above the eclectic mix of hardened professionals, dissatisfied conscripts and 'skeleton' units awaiting reservists on mobilization that represented the Soviet army. They had the most advanced equipment, they took their pick of the best recruits, they were disproportionately staffed by professional soldiers and, on the whole, were predominantly made up of Slavs. They were elite and they knew it, and it was this combination of esprit de corps and combat readiness which has ensured that they have become the seedcorns for the new national armies. There are three main reasons for Russia's dependence upon the special forces:

■ **Quality over quantity**. With the armed forces being steadily reduced, the need is currently for smaller forces able to do the job of larger armies thanks to their mobility, flexibility and professionalism. In Lenin's words, 'better fewer, but better'. At a time when the regular forces are in crisis, it makes sense to use and develop those elements which have survived the collapse of the Soviet state in good shape. The heavy bias towards staffing them with Slavs also means that Russia has a substantial cadre of experienced professionals at its disposal.

■ **Flexibility**. They are best suited to the real threats likely to face the Russian state. These threats will come not from conventional foreign aggression but local brushfire wars such as in Chechnya and border clashes. The new military doctrine will also mean that the army will be called on to intervene or keep the peace in the neighbouring countries of

Figure 13.1: Russian special and intervention forces

Unit	Base	Military District
VDV — AIR ASSAULT FORCES		
7th Guards Airborne Division	Novorossiisk	North Caucasus
76th Guards Airborne Division	Pskov	Leningrad
98th Guards Airborne Division	Ivanovo	Moscow
104th Guards Airborne Division	Ulyanovsk	Volga
106th Guards Airborne Division	Tula	Moscow
242nd Training Centre	Omsk	Ural
117th Independent Communications Brigade	Medvezhi Ozera	Moscow
218th VDV *Spetsnaz* Battalion	Medvezhi Ozera	Moscow
DShV — ASSAULT-LANDING TROOPS		
11th Independent Assault-Landing Brigade	Ulan Ude	Transbaikal
13th Independent Assault-Landing Brigade	Magdagachi	Far East
21st Independent Assault-Landing Brigade	Stavropol	North Caucasus
36th Independent Assault-Landing Brigade	Garbolovo	Volga
37th Independent Assault-Landing Brigade	Chernyakovsk	(Kaliningrad)
56th Guards Independent Assault-Landing Brigade	Volgodonsk	North Caucasus
83rd Independent Assault-Landing Brigade	Ussuriisk	Far East
SPETSNAZ		
2nd Brigade	Pskov	Leningrad
3rd Brigade	Samara	Urals
12th Brigade	Lagodekhi	Transcaucasus
14th Brigade	Ussuriisk	Far East
16th Brigade	Chuchkovo	Moscow
22nd Brigade	Aksai	North Caucasus
24th Brigade	Kyakhta	Transbaikal
67th Brigade	Berdsk	Siberian
1071st Training Regiment	Pechori	Leningrad
MOBILE FORCES (see Figure 13.2)		
NAVAL INFANTRY		
Naval Infantry brigade	Murmansk	Northern Fleet
63rd Guards Naval Infantry Brigade	Pechenga	Northern Fleet
Naval *Spetsnaz* brigade	Murmansk	Northern Fleet
Naval Infantry division	Vladivostok	Pacific Fleet
Naval *Spetsnaz* brigade	Vladivostok	Pacific Fleet
Naval Infantry regiment	Sevastopol	Black Sea Fleet
Naval *Spetsnaz* brigade	Sevastopol	Black Sea Fleet
Naval Infantry brigade	Kaliningrad	Baltic Fleet
Naval *Spetsnaz* brigade	Baltiisk	Baltic Fleet
PEACEKEEPING FORCES		
27th Guards Motor Rifle Division	Totskoye	Volga
45th Motor Rifle Division	Kamenka	Leningrad

the 'Near Abroad', a job which calls for specialized units which can be deployed at short notice *(see Chapter 3)*.

■ **Service loyalties**. Russia's first defence minister, Pavel Grachev, was a paratrooper. He brought with him a determination both to protect his former arm of service and shake up the old Soviet orthodoxies, with their dependence upon massed tank attacks. Although he has proved a very poor minister, he has been able to shift resources to the special and intervention forces. He has also created plans for the Mobile Forces (MS) which — if they are ever realized — would make them the core of the Russian army.

THE AIRBORNE FORCES

Soviet interest in *desant* operations — special force assaults or landings in depth — had a sound historical pedigree. The Red Army was the first to experiment with paratroop units, with small groups dropped in the campaign against Central Asian rebels in 1929. In the Second World War, the Airborne Landing Troops (VDV — *Vozdushno-desantnye voiska*) were used more often as infantry than paratroopers. A combination of a lack of transport aircraft, bad luck and poor planning meant that most of their combat drops proved disastrous failures. Although there seemed a real chance that the VDV might even be disbanded, a combination of new technologies and new problems brought them back to the fore by the late 1950s. The USSR had begun to develop aircraft able to make credible drops, while more powerful weapons and light vehicles gave them a real punch. In the 1956 suppression of the Hungarian uprising, they were largely used as shock ground troops. By the 1968 invasion of Czechoslovakia, though, their real potential had been realized and it was the 'blue berets' of the 103rd Guards Airborne Division which seized Prague in a surprise attack. The invasion of Afghanistan in 1979 was similarly led by the VDV.

The paratroop divisions of the VDV were thus amongst the elite of the Soviet armed forces. As such, they were predominantly made up of Slavs, notably Russians and Ukrainians. With the collapse of the USSR, the Slav republics divided the VDV amongst themselves. Ukraine received three brigades of paratroopers, essentially the 98th Division minus some of its support assets. The 103rd 'Vitebsk' Division has been transferred to Belarusian control, along with the Independent Airborne Brigade at Brest. Five divisions were left to Russia. On paper, each is 6750 strong, although the VDV may have suffered from the under-manning which is endemic to the rest of the armed forces. Three paratroop regiments make up the division's core, along with an artillery regiment, an air defence battalion, engineers and other support troops. All told, the division disposes of 318 airborne combat vehicles (BMDs), 72 *Nona* self-propelled mortars and another thousand trucks, jeeps and combat vehicles.

The VDV will remain at the forefront of the Russian military, even if the age of the large-scale parachute drop seems to be over. They have continued to experiment with new means of airborne insertion, from microlight gliders to 'stealthy' new helicopters. More to the point, they provide Moscow a tough and reliable assault force whose troopers are motivated by a proud history and a self-conscious sense of elite. Some 12 VDV battalions saw action in the invasion of Chechnya, amounting to around a division. Paratroopers remain at the heart of most of the developments taking place in the Russian army, from professionalization to the formation of rapid-deployment and peacekeeping forces. In the words of Colonel General Yevgeni Podkolzin, their commander since 1992, the airborne troops are 'the most highly mobile and powerful arm of the armed forces', serving Russia 'from Novorossiisk on the Black Sea to the shores of the Pacific'.

THE HELICOPTER CAVALRY

The age of the helicopter brought a new force onto the Soviet order of battle. The USSR's first airmobile brigades were formed in the early 1970s but these were little more than infantrymen given a little extra training in helicopter insertion. The real need was for units rather more closely integrated with helicopter forces and able to respond quickly and in strength to changing situations. As a result, so-called 'Special Designation Brigades' were established in the late 1970s. These were later redesignated DShB *(Desantno-shturmovaya brigada)*, commonly rendered as 'air-assault brigade' but more accurately 'assault-landing brigade'.

Just as the paratroopers of the VDV represent a strategic-level rapid deployment force, the DShB was conceived to provide front and army commanders with mobile and flexible forces for a variety of purposes, from seizing bridgeheads to blocking enemy counterattacks. The war in Afghanistan provided the DShB with a range of challenges which bred new tactics, new equipment and a new respect for the flexibility and tempo of heliborne operations. Whereas before they were primarily regarded as an adjunct to conventional forces, they were increasingly seen as a replacement. Most Soviet forces in Afghanistan were restricted to garrison and convoy duties but the DShB could take the war to the rebels. Platoons or companies were generally kept on round-the-clock alert, ready to repel surprise attacks or respond quickly to tips from scouts or spies.

By the end of the Afghan war, there were some 10 DShBs, along with at least as many independent assault-landing battalions. These forces were transferred almost intact into the Russian army, although a cut in the size of the armed forces and a lack of helicopters has led to a reduction to seven DShBs, supplemented by smaller assault-landing battalions. Each DShB is built around three battalions, of which one is fully parachute-trained and equipped. The brigade is allocated a full helicopter transport regiment of one heavy lift squadron (21 Mi-26 'Halo') and 2-3 squadrons of Mi-8/17 (21 helicopters per squadron). This is sufficient to lift about half the brigade in one sortie but, on the whole, assault-landing troops are deployed in company or battalion-strength units. The independent battalions similarly comprise three companies.

DShB and airmobile operations are by no means cheap but there is a strong lobby for the helicopter cavalry in Moscow. There has even been talk of designating them as an entirely separate arm of service, the Assault-landing Troops (DShV — *Desantno-shturmovaya voiska*). On the one hand, they evolve with technology. As helicopters become more advanced and are supplemented by new aircraft such as tilt-rotors (which combine many of the best features of the conventional aeroplane and a helicopter), so too will the DShB become more versatile. The war of the future, after all, will be an increasingly three-dimensional phenomenon. Besides which, although the DShBs were originally intended to operate on the fluid high-tempo battlefield of a future potential war with NATO or China, they are also clearly valuable assets in any low-intensity conflicts.

THE NAVAL INFANTRY

Although the USSR never developed anything like the seaborne army which is the US Marine Corps, its Naval Infantry *(Morskaya piekhota)* was heir to a distinct role and history. Sailors from the tsarist navy had been among the first soldiers of the Bolshevik Revolution. While the Soviets concentrated on land power, the Naval Infantry distinguished themselves in the Second World War. Sailors were pressed hurriedly into service in a series of operations in the Baltic and the Black Sea.

In 1947, the Naval Infantry were largely disbanded, some remaining as Coastal Defence Forces, but they were reformed in 1961. Although not as prestigious or skilled as the paratroopers, the 14 000-strong Naval Infantry corps could also be counted among the elite of the old Soviet military. They were used to operating in relatively small units, seizing beachheads and raiding along the coastline, and many were parachute-qualified or trained in landing by helicopter or hovercraft. Their black berets and striped naval t-shirts (which were also adopted by the VDV) carried with them a certain combat tradition.

Consequently, Moscow also made sure that it retained almost all of them. All the Naval Infantry except for the Black Sea Fleet's 810th Independent

Naval Infantry Brigade (lost to Ukraine) now come under Russian command. Each of Russia's four fleets has its own force of marines. The Northern Fleet has two 3000-strong brigades, the Baltic one, the Pacific a 7000-strong division and the Black Sea Fleet a 2000-strong regiment. In addition, each fleet commands a 1000-strong brigade of Naval Special Designation Troops (*Spetsnaz — Spetsial'novo naznacheniya*) and a company of long-range reconnaissance Naval *Spetsnaz*.

THE MOBILE FORCES

As already mentioned, Defence Minister Grachev announced in 1992 an entirely new concept for the Russian armed forces. Instead of being based around heavy mechanized and armoured divisions, the Russian army would be divided between local defensive units which would largely be 'skeleton' units ready to be brought up to strength in time of war by a mobilization of reservists, and a rapid-deployment intervention corps, the Mobile Forces (MS).

On paper, the rationale was compelling. Russia could not afford huge armies ready for war on every front and the MS could quickly meet any threat and, if not repel it, then at least delay it long enough for general mobilization. The army also had to be ready to restore order or impose Moscow's writ in the 'Near Abroad', requiring intervention forces rather more mobile, flexible and professional than the run of the mill Russian conscript. Besides, it fitted into the 'paratrooperization' of the High Command under Grachev. The VDV would form 60 per cent of the MS, along with associated elements from the Military Transport Aviation.

With a total projected strength of around 100 000, the MS would be a powerful strategic-level asset whose deployment would be at the discretion of the defence minister and commander-in-chief (the president). Kept at a high level of readiness, MS units would be ready for any of a wide range of contingencies. These could range from insurrections and bush wars to natural disasters and, presumably, the evacuation or protection of ethnic Russians in other republics. It would be further divided into two forces:

■ **Immediate Reaction Force.** The Immediate Reaction Force (SNR — *Sily nemedlennovo reagirovaniya*) would be the first on the scene in any crisis. Made up of light highly mobile forces, the SNR should ready to move within 24 hours of an alert. It would largely be comprised of paratroopers, DShB and light mechanized forces. These could be deployed quickly and deliver a powerful initial punch with the assistance of their air cover, even if lacking the tanks and munitions for prolonged operations.

Figure 13.2: The Mobile Forces (MS)

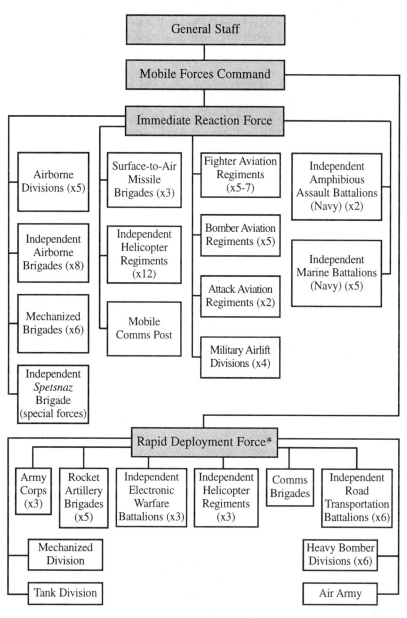

* Apparently not operationally subordinate to the MS Command during peacetime.
Source: *Krasnaya zvezda*, 18 December 1992, p 2.

■ **Rapid Deployment Force**. Following on the heels of the SNR, the Rapid Deployment Force (SBR — *Sily bystrovo razvyortyvaniya*) would then provide the heavy support it lacked. It would comprise three army corps, equivalent to about five divisions, ready to be deployed within three to seven days.

In abstract, the MS concept is a radical and imaginative solution to Russia's defence needs. In practice, it is ludicrously unrealistic. These sorts of 'power projection' forces need to be highly skilled and, yet, the Defence Ministry is having to rely increasingly upon under-trained and reluctant conscripts. They require a whole array of expensive training centres, transport aircraft and supply bases but the military budget scarcely stretches to keeping existing forces fed and clothed. While the units which would make up the MS exist, in various degrees of combat readiness, there is little real prospect of them being unified into such a rapid deployment force in any meaningful sense.

SPETSNAZ: ELITE WITHIN AN ELITE

The Special Designation Troops are the Russian special forces, although the contraction *Spetsnaz* has been used, often inaccurately, to cover a variety of different forces. Since the 1960s, Soviet military intelligence (GRU) maintained a number of *Spetsnaz* brigades. Popular myth has made them into superheroic assassins and polyglot saboteurs but their subordination to the GRU underlines their main function, namely intelligence. *Spetsnaz* could be used for commando raids, especially against such key targets as nuclear-missile sites and command centres. However, their main function was to supplement and support the spy satellites, reconnaissance drones, electronic information-gathering stations and the other technological services available to a modern intelligence agency. In time of war, they would range up to and behind enemy lines, monitor troop movements, capture prisoners for interrogation and perhaps also spread some chaos and mayhem on their way. Similarly, the Naval *Spetsnaz* brigades attached to the fleets would reconnoitre beaches before landings and sabotage enemy ships and harbours. For these missions, they had an impressive array of gadgets, from mini-submarines and portable nuclear bombs to underwater rifles and anti-frogman grenade launchers.

The *Spetsnaz* are composed predominantly of conscripts, albeit selected for their unusually high quality and military aptitude. Although there are some all-professional 'elite within an elite' units, the *Spetsnaz* overall are broadly analogous to the British Paras or US Rangers rather than the SAS or SEAL commandos. The Soviets maintained 10 *Spetsnaz* brigades, each of around 1000 soldiers, along with small companies of 110 men attached to each all-arms or tank army. Eight of the brigades remain under Russian control, although the largest, the 5th 'Marina Gora' Brigade was lost to Belarus and the 10th Brigade to Ukraine. All four Naval *Spetsnaz* brigades were transferred to Russian command, though there are reports which suggest that several are well below their established strength of around 900. *Spetsnaz* from the 22nd Brigade participated, albeit rather reluctantly, in the Chechen operation, while some from the 16th Brigade were involved in the October Coup in 1993.

To a large extent, though, the *Spetsnaz* are at the moment in the doldrums. The real need is not for military scouts but the sort of anti-terrorist and police commando squads discussed in Chapter 11. While well trained and well armed, the *Spetsnaz* are not first and foremost designed for this sort of mission. Besides, they are disinclined to become glorified SWAT teams and the internal security agencies themselves do not want to let the military take over their new-found role. Nevertheless, the 'grey wolves' (after their new unit badge) represent a powerful and flexible asset and it is hard to believe Moscow will let them go to waste.

PEACEKEEPING FORCES

One of the potentially important roles Russian special and intervention forces may play is as peacekeepers within the terms agreed at the CIS Summit in July 1992. These collective peacekeeping forces are mandated to act as military cease-fire and disengagement observers. The peacekeepers are meant to be volunteers (though this guideline is frequently broken) and are distinguished by their white helmets marked with a blue band.

However, these operations are often based on a muddled understanding of what 'peacekeeping' really means or are just a flag of convenience for Russian military interventions *(see Chapter 8)*. A particular problem is that few Russian troops have the morale, professionalism or training such missions require. Two divisions have been formally assigned a peacekeeping role: the 27th Guards Motor Rifle Division at Totskoye; and the 45th Motor Rifle Division at Kamenka, near St Petersburg. These are being reconfigured for their new role, losing much of their heavy equipment and armour for the light armoured vehicles and jeeps more appropriate for peacekeepers and receiving training in deconfliction, patrolling and liaison. In many cases, though, peacekeeping duties have simply been allocated to whichever unit was available. The force which moved into South Ossetia in July 1992, for example, was made up of a battalion from the 104th Regiment of the 76th Airborne Division, Russian Interior Army troops, elements of the Georgian National Guard and North Ossetian soldiers. In Moldova, the peacekeeping

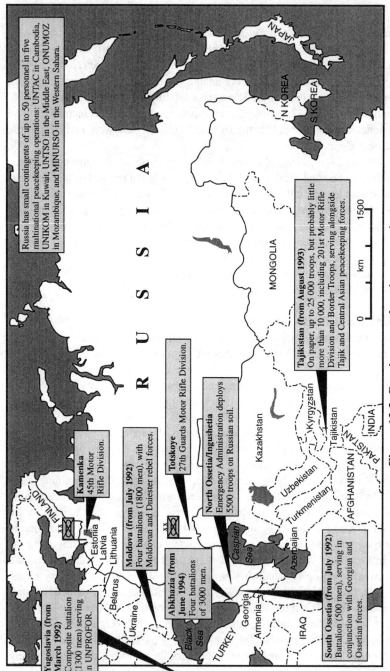

Russia has small contingents of up to 50 personnel in five multinational peacekeeping operations: UNTAC in Cambodia, UNIKOM in Kuwait, UNTSO in the Middle East, ONUMOZ in Mozambique, and MINURSO in the Western Sahara.

Kamenka 45th Motor Rifle Division.

Moldova (from July 1992) Four battalions (1800 men), with Moldovan and Dniester rebel forces.

Totskoye 27th Guards Motor Rifle Division.

North Ossetia/Ingushetia Emergency Administration deploys 5500 troops on Russian soil.

Tajikistan (from August 1993) On paper, up to 25 000 troops, but probably little more than 10 000, including 201st Motor Rifle Division and Border Troops, serving alongside Tajik and Central Asian peacekeeping forces.

Abkhazia (from June 1994) Four battalions of 3000 men.

South Ossetia (from July 1992) Battalion (500 men), serving in conjunction with Georgian and Ossetian forces.

Yugoslavia (from March 1992) Composite battalion (1300 men) serving in UNPROFOR.

Figure 13.3: Russian peacekeeping operations

task force included the 137th Regiment of the 106th Guards Airborne Division, another from the 76th Guards Airborne Division and two battalions each from Moldovan and Dniester forces. To date, Russian peacekeeping operations have brought very mixed results. By virtue of their size and their preparedness to impose peace of a sort by heavy-handed military action, they have brought a cessation of hostilities to Moldova, Ossetia and, to a lesser extent, Abkhazia in Georgia. In Tajikistan, though, they are really belligerents in a civil war rather than neutral peacekeepers. They have also a very dubious record as members of the UNPROFOR force in Yugoslavia. There, the Russian battalion (RUSBAT) has acquired a reputation for pro-Serbian partiality and wholesale black marketeering that bodes ill for any future Russian deployments. Good peacekeeping forces, after all, are expensive and specialized. Semi-trained conscripts and underpaid professionals will not be up to the task, especially as long as the Russians continue to confuse neutral peacemaking with the imposition of Moscow's writ upon a troubled region. The dilemma for the Russian government is that perennial one: money. Peacekeepers, like the Mobile Forces, like the internal security armies, like so many other items on Moscow's shopping list, cost money. To date, the Russians have failed either to come up with ways to meet the total bill or to reach any clear decision as to where their priorities lie. The result is the usual messy compromise: doing everything badly on a shoestring rather than doing fewer things right.

14 Agendas for Russia's Future

A maxim for Kremlin watchers in the 1980s was that, if in doubt, it was always safest to be pessimistic: the USSR usually lived down to expectations. Post-Soviet Russia has often seemed eager to adopt the same criteria. Perhaps a useful way of trying to reach some useful and usable conclusions about Russia's future course, though, would be first to consider some of the broad and often conceptual dilemmas facing her.

THE ECONOMIC AGENDA

Can the Russian economy be stabilized?

The answer is, of course, eventually that it can — but when and at what cost? The lesson from the post-Soviet and Warsaw Pact states seems to be that a leadership made up almost exclusively of reconditioned ex-Party bosses need not be a serious obstacle if the political, economic and social preconditions for modernity are there. The Czech Republic, Hungary, and even in its own dependent way, Belarus, can attest to that. However, if they are not, then no amount of radical rhetoric, Western aid or glossy public relations will make up for their lack. A key problem is that existing attitudes and structures need to be deconstructed before they can be replaced. Far too much effort and scarce resources are being extended on holding on to the old ways. To some extent, this can be explained by political factors; cutting subsidies to loss-making industries, for example, could create mass unemployment and thus risk a social explosion. Nevertheless, stability is slowly coming to the Russian economy.

What sort of economy will it be?

Although there is little likelihood of a renewed swing towards authoritarian-statist methods, authoritarian state-driven capitalist reconstruction, consciously looking to South Korea, Singapore and China for inspiration, is quite conceivable. The state would guarantee strategically targeted investment and a docile workforce, looking to woo foreign investors with the promise of cheap labour and new markets with cheap goods. By 1995, it became increasingly clear that the Russian economy was evolving in a way reminiscent of the Soviet era. Where once the dominant forces were Party and government bureaucracies and defence-industrial enterprises, the new players are finance-industrial groups, privatized monopolies and other powerful corporate entities. The dominant powers are key banks and the energy sector (notably *Gazprom*, the natural gas giant, and the petrochemicals combine *Lukoil*). Although much is still to be done, it is clear that Soviet traditions of building big and monopolistically live on. The future of the Russian economy appears to be divided between energetic entrepreneurs operating at the grass roots and huge corporate cartels, often operating all across the former USSR, at the other extreme, with very little middle ground.

Can the economy be demilitarized?

Even by 1995, the military-industrial complex accounts for almost six million Russian jobs, including those of almost two-thirds of all scientists and technicians. While this might suggest an urgent need to shift the balance of the economy towards civil production, it is regularly held up as one of the few industries which really can compete for world markets. In the first quarter of 1995, admittedly an unusually good three months, the state arms cartel *Rosvooruzheniye* announced deals worth US$1500 million. Besides which, the military are eager to preserve a large domestic arms industry, not least to ensure that they have the necessary capacity if they ever have to tool up for a major war. The question is thus in a way whether Russia will ever want to demilitarize.

THE POLITICAL AGENDA

What will happen after Yeltsin departs the political scene?

Boris Yeltsin's worsening health and political standing make it very unlikely he will long remain in office. In July 1995, he was hospitalized as suffering from ischaemia, a diminution of the flow of blood and oxygen to the heart as a result of blocked arteries. As his stay in hospital was extended, it soon became clear that the problems were rather more serious. An old picture of him was even issued in a clumsy and unsuccessful attempt to portray him as on the mend before it was admitted that he had suffered a heart attack. Yeltsin's constitution has been fragile for years. He drinks heavily, he takes cortisone for a back condition and, reportedly, suffers from arteriosclerosis. His political health is scarcely any better and his wife, Naina, is understandably concerned that he should not stand for re-election out of a fear that he would not be up to the rigours of the campaign trail. Many within his inner circle, gripped by a sense of fin de secle, are setting themselves up suitable bolt-holes for a future after Yeltsin whether in commerce, in politics or in academe. Yet, the current regime is not a personal dictatorship but an alliance of powerful regional, economic and political forces. The most likely prospect is of another member of this elite rising to fill Yeltsin's place — probably Prime Minister Chernomyrdin — and continuing to manage the country in the interests of this alliance. There is, after all, a striking degree of consensus within Russian politics about the importance of protecting national interests and strategic primacy within the post-Soviet 'Near Abroad' and the need for a slow transition to a market economy, albeit one dominated by major combines with close links to the state (and, hardly coincidentally, the new business-political elite). All central parties also have to live with the realities of Russia's fragmentation into semi-autonomous regional fiefdoms. A new president will thus probably not change matters. This may be the ultimate irony of Yeltsin's career; by his actions, he destroyed the USSR but his role in the creation of the new Russia may prove to have been so marginal that his loss will scarcely be noticed.

Will Russian democracy survive?

To put it another way, can Russian democracy be established? As discussed in Chapter 4, Russian democracy is a particularly distinctive and fragile example of the species. Democracy does not just mean granting the masses the right to vote; after all, even Soviet citizens had that. It also requires genuine choice between candidates, open and pluralistic media, individual social and economic freedoms and overall a participation of the people in the public life of the nation. While Russia has the forms of a republic, it still needs to develop the strong civil society which is at the heart of any working democracy.

Will the Russian state survive?

The regional and ethnic pressures upon the unity of the federation discussed in Chapter 5 will need resolution if the state is to survive. This may be by co-optation and confederation. Alternatively, the state may adopt more decisive measures. One proposal raised in 1993-94, for example, was to encourage a new wave of internal migration, a strategic resettlement of ethnic Russians displaced from other nations or those living in distant industrial centres facing closure. Some five million would, according to this plan, be encouraged to move to Central Russia, with the promise of farmland and building materials, while a similar number settled in Siberia and another million in the Far East. At a stroke, this would dilute local ethnic minorities, offer some future to unemployed workers and demobilized soldiers and stimulate the rise of a new class of *kulaks*, prosperous yeomen farmers.

THE GEOPOLITICAL AGENDA

European or Asian?

The debate over Russia's place in the world, discussed in Chapter 9, has yet to be completed. At times, Russia appears to see herself as a part of the European/North Atlantic world. It certainly shares certain cultural roots, although these never really recovered from the centuries of Mongol domination in the Middle Ages. When Europe went through its Reformation and laid the foundations for a liberal individualist society, Russia was still locked in a collective Asiatic mould. There are still huge cultural divisions between Russia and Europe, and this new state must still come to terms with its identity and its interests in the world.

Is there anything the outside world can and should do?

Although there is ample scope for outsiders to worsen Russia's predicament, there is ultimately little that can positively be done. In the economic sector, efforts have been made to introduce modern methods and skills but they have proven futile when there is not the will to apply them. No end of visits from Western bankers, for example, have yet managed to establish a working and honest clearing bank system. Endless amounts of aid could be poured into and lost in Russia without any real return.

Perhaps the best thing the outside world can do is to avoid being either inconsistent or indulgent. There are no painless short cuts to financial discipline, economic dynamism or political stability. Nor can Russia be allowed to feel it has special rights in Central and Eastern Europe or the 'Near Abroad'. Not only does this encourage 'New Imperialism' at home, but it also denies the other nations of the region their basic sovereignty.

THE HISTORICAL AGENDA

Empire or Federation?

Russians have yet to come to terms with their imperial past. They may not have benefited much from Moscow's domination over non-Russians during the tsarist and Soviet eras but this state has always been an empire. Ultimately, Russians will have either to develop a new relationship with the other ethnic groups within their state or accept a future spent pacifying and suppressing them. Empires last and evolve when even their subject peoples can find something within for them, whether the proud boast that *cives Romanus sum* or the pageantry and order of the Raj. Without that often very temporary bond, though, they will fall, and rarely peaceably.

First World or Third?

The conceit of a Soviet 'Second World', between the industrialized 'First' and developing 'Third', was always rather artificial. The question that remains is which parts of the old USSR will manage to claw their way into the developed world. Belarus and the Baltic states seem to have a good chance, possibly even Ukraine. Since the late Soviet era, Transcaucasia has been less a geographical term, more a war correspondent's playground. Nevertheless, some minimal peace may be on the way. Even so, these are not nations with an imminently rosy future. The nations of Central Asia, once they have either reconciled themselves to their boundaries or developed into a new constellation of genuine nation-states, could become useful and dynamic members of the developing world community. So what about Russia? The gibe that the USSR was nothing more than 'Upper Volta with rockets' was always patently untrue; no nation with that reservoir of skills, industry and resources and world-class science and technology could so easily be categorized. Much the same is true of Russia, yet as the veneer of a modern superpower wears ever thinner, it is possible to see the poverty of the old Russia behind it ever more clearly. Yet can Russia live with a future not amongst the mighty world powers?

Will Russia follow traditional patterns?

Russian history has traditionally been defined by cycles of reform and reaction. Attempts to modernize the state lead to political liberalization; ensuing internal instability triggers a return to authoritarian conservatism. In many ways, Yeltsin's Russia risks becoming the reactionary successor to Gorbachev's reforms. If history can be used as a predictive tool, then Russia's past suggests a future of increasingly oppressive and autocratic rule.

A LOOK TO THE TWENTY-FIRST CENTURY

It may thus be worth concluding with an entirely speculative glance at some potential futures facing Russia. Without pretending to any particular originality or prescience, three possible outcomes come to mind as being worth investigation:

Scenario 1: 'Imperial Russia'

'Imperial Russia' would probably not be an empire as such, although the return of the tsar as head of state and constitutional monarch is far from improbable. Above all, it would be an authoritarian state with an adventurist desire to impose Russian hegemony over Eurasia and thus both extend national prestige and vent internal pressures through jingoism. Traditional patterns of ruling Russia would reassert themselves, with a powerful oligarchy bringing together key interest groups. They would be held together by a charismatic and forceful leader, less a dictator and more an able 'chairman of the board', brokering deals and establishing consensus amongst them. Whether based in Moscow or St Petersburg, this regime would draw selectively upon both its tsarist and Soviet past. Like both, it would assert its control over the regions of Russia by a combination of the co-optation of local elites and the ruthless suppression of any signs of local independence, through the political police, military and specialized security forces.

Large parts of the economy would be in private ownership, but the state would control a wide range of economically strategic sectors such as communications and the armaments industries. There would also be much scope for 'shadow nationalization': once cartels or major firms reach a certain level of importance, they would be brought within the ruling oligarchy. Foreign economic influence would be treated with great suspicion, and foreign investment limited and monitored, largely out of fear that it undermines the power of the centre.

There would be little scope for individual political choice under this regime, although opportunities for ambitious and effective Russians prepared to 'play by the rules' to go far. Society would be controlled and stratified, with a distinct ruling class made up of government officials, army officers and others useful to the regime, as well as successful managers and entrepreneurs. Only slowly would this rigidify into a distinct class but there would be a strong pressure towards exclusivity, visible in a desire to use honorific titles (quite possibly aristocratic), decorations, perhaps uniforms and privileges, to mark out the new class. Private schools and universities, as well as nepotism and 'old boy networks', would thrive as a means of making this class hereditary. Russians would decidedly remain the imperial race, and make up — with co-opted local collaborators — the governors, administrators, policemen, officers, head teachers and key managers in non-Russian areas. Despite a myth of unity beneath the state, the regime would cultivate nationalism and xenophobia, and seek to impose the Russian language and values upon its subjects. The Russian Orthodox Church would become increasingly powerful and influential, raising the spectre of 'underground religion' as a force around which resistance could coalesce, whether Islam in the south or Catholicism in an occupied western Ukraine.

The key problems facing any such regime would be to maintain the balance between stability and stagnation and avoid over-stretch. A population used to a diet of bread and circuses would expect the national glories to continue. A military establishment built for empire would need to justify retaining its budgets. As new areas come under Russian domination, they would carry with them new headaches of control and security. Perhaps the best model is to be found in the British conquest of India. As each new area was brought under informal control, this upset local power relationships and created generated resistance which soon came to threaten British influence. Facing a choice of a humiliating withdrawal or the armed imposition of formal control, the former prevailed. A new region brought under the crown meant yet another border to police, new neighbouring regions over which to assert informal influence and a new administrative structure to establish. 'Imperial Russia' would probably not survive that long — but its collapse would be both brutal and bloody.

Scenario 2: Working Russia
The most positive likely future for Russia hinges around its ability to shake off the psychological, political and territorial legacies of its tsarist and Soviet past, such that it can begin afresh and create a liberal capitalist and democratic system from scratch. Such a regime would probably combine a manageable central administration with strong local government, perhaps akin to American states though German *Länder* are probably better examples. This would almost certainly entail a contraction of Russian borders to a *Rus'* heartland. This Russia, then, would be less of a multi-ethnic empire and more a large but manageable nation state, within which 'healthy' patriotism could replace the exploitative and exclusive nationalism of empire. This streamlined Russia would include European Russia to and beyond the Urals, and probably extend into western Siberia as far as Lake Baikal. Its southern border would reach Volgograd. Although this region would include ethnic enclaves, notably Komi and the collection of indigenous regions around Tatarstan, the immigration of ethnic Russians from the Far East as well as northern Kazakhstan, Central Asia, the Far East and other regions, would help both populate the thinly settled northern agricultural regions and permit a greater dilution of the non-Russians.

The central government would comprise a president and prime minister, with the former very much the more powerful, possibly also with a constitutional and symbolic tsar, and a parliament reflecting both national and regional opinion. The shrinkage of Russia would bring with it key advantages: consolidation into a more defensible unit, shorter and more defensible frontiers, the shedding of regions with large populations of potential fifth columnists and, it is supposed, a more stable economy. Ukraine, once a very distant second, would become a rival on a rather more even footing, as will the traditional enemy, Poland. Russia would assiduously court Europe, hoping that by shedding much of its territory and aspirations east of the Urals it had become a viable and non-threatening partner.

This is, of course, the most optimistic — and, arguably, least credible —

projection. It would entail Russia coming to terms with herself and her geopolitical position. She would not be an advanced industrial Western country, nor would she be of Asia. Ultimately, Russia would have chosen to develop slowly as a backward but earnest and obliging second cousin to Europe and North America, turning her back on dreams of a mighty Eurasian empire and a new sphere of influence to her south and east.

Scenario 3: Decaying Russia

There is no reason to expect dramatic upsets and developments in Russia. Perhaps the most likely scenario postulates a steady decay of the Russian Federation into a large and diffuse developing world mixed-economy nation. It would have a notionally powerful executive government which, nonetheless, has little effective power in the regions and which are, instead, dominated by local cliques, mafia groupings, charismatic politicians and self interest groups. The country would become steadily more heterogeneous, with many regions as well as interest groups seizing de facto autonomy, and the divides between rich and poor regions and rich and poor citizens alike opening wider still. A nation such as Brazil is, in some ways, a good example in that it possesses some industries and areas up to the standards of the developed world, yet it also a massive hinterland of poverty and backwardness. So too would Russia present a varied picture of advanced theoretical science in the research laboratories of the sophisticated metropola of Moscow and St Petersburg, while out in the countryside, as the spare parts for the tractors became too expensive and the collective farm buildings crumbled, the peasants return to the horse-drawn plough and wooden huts. The central government would be powerfully presidential in form, if still probably oligarchic in content, and severely limited by the weakness of the government and, by extension, the power of autonomous interest groups and the regions.

With most of the economy outside state control, and an end to the practical authority of the state, Russian society would to a large extent be atomized and thus politically quiescent. A sluggish and perennially crisis-hit economy, high unemployment and erratic state welfare services, as well as widespread alienation from a discredited political process, would serve instead to create a society built around the grass-roots loyalties of family and region, a continued rise in organized crime and huge differentials between rich and poor regions, individuals and kin-groups.

Such a Russian Federation would be not predator but prey. The main danger it would pose the rest of the world (except as a haven for international organized crime) would be as a source of chaos and thus temptation. While clinging to its seat on the UN Security Council, this Russia would have abandoned most of its global pretences, and its foreign policy priorities would be to secure foreign aid and investment and avert threats to its survival. It would be a wheeler-dealing plaintiff, ever looking to sell its UN vote to cultivate friends. Whether this is Europe, the USA or Japan is irrelevant; the point is, could there be some immediate gain for Russia in it? Its military forces would decay into impotence. A small central cadre may remain, little more than a praetorian force to protect the Moscow-St Petersburg heartland and, from time to time, rattle a sabre at some region which oversteps the mark in its disrespect for the government. Beyond this, most regions would have paramilitary forces which would vary immensely in size and quality. More assertive regions such as Siberia and Tatarstan might choose to establish relatively effective forces as a symbol of their autonomy — and, implicitly, as a warning to Moscow — whereas, elsewhere, these units might be little more than the gunmen of the dominant local mafias given pseudo-legitimacy or a handful of ill-disciplined vigilantes.

The reader is entirely free to pick his or her favoured outcome. All that can be said with any confidence is that Russia has in her time been weak and she has been powerful, she has been conquered and she has been a conqueror. She has never been predictable, though, and nor has she ever been irrelevant.

GLOSSARY

Russian abbreviations used in the text

AFB   *Agenstevo federalnoi bezopasnosti* — Federal Security Agency

DShB   *Desantno-shturmovaya brigada* — Assault-landing Brigade

DShV   *Desantno-shturmovaya voiska* — Assault-landing Troops

FAPSI   *Federalnoi agenstvo pravitelstvennoi svyazi i informatsiy* — Federal Agency for Government Communications and Information

FSB   *Federal'naya sluzhba bezopasnosti* — Federal Security Service

FSG   *Federal'naya sluzhba granitsy* — Federal Border Service

FSK   *Federal'naya sluzhba kontrrazvedki* — Federal Counter-intelligence Service

GAI   *Gosudarstvennaya avtomobil'naya inspektsiya* — State Automobile Inspectorate

GKChP   *Gosudarstvenny komitet chrezvychainovo polzheniya* — State Committee for the State of Emergency

GNR   *Gruppa nemedlennovo reagirovanniya* — Rapid Reaction Group

GRU   *Glavnoye razvedyvatelnoye upravleniye* — Chief Intelligence Directorate

GUO   *Glavnoye upravleniye okhrany* — Chief Guard Directorate

KGB   *Komitet gosudarstvennoi bezopasnosti* — Committee of State Security

KOGG   *Komitet po okhrane gosudarstvennoi granitsy* — Committee for the Protection of the State Border

KPRF   *Kommunisticheskaya partiya Rossiiskoi federatsii* — Communist Party of the Russian Federation

MB   *Ministerstvo bezopasnosti* — Security Ministry

MEK   *Mezhdunarodnyi ekonomicheskii komitet* — Inter-state Economic Committee

MOB   *Militsiya obshchestvennoi bezopasnosti* — Public Security Militia

MP   *Morskaya piekhota* — Naval Infantry

MS   *Mobilnye sily* — Mobile Forces

MUR   *Moskovskii ugolovnyi rozysk* — Criminal Investigations Directorate

MVD   *Ministerstvo vnutrennykh del* — Ministry of Internal Affairs

NP	*Nalogovaya politsiya* — Tax Police
ODON	*Otdeleniya diviziya osobennovo naznacheniya* — Independent Special Designation Division
OMON	*Otryad militsii osobennovo naznacheniya* — Special Designation Police Detachment
OMSN	*Otryad militsii spetsial'novo naznacheniya* — Specialized Designation Police Detachment
Opnaz	*Operativnoe naznacheniya* — Operational Designation Forces
PGU	*Pervoye glavnoye upravleniye* — First Chief Directorate (of the KGB)
PPS	*Patrul'no-postovaya sluzhba* — Patrol-Guard Service
PV	*Pogranichnye voiska* — Border Troops
SBP	*Sluzhba bezopasnosti prezidenta* — Presidential Security Service
SBR	*Sily bystrovo razvyortyvaniya* — Rapid Deployment Force
SKVO	*Srednyi kavkazskyi voennyi okrug* — North Caucasian Military District
SMBM	*Spetsial'nyi motorizovannyi batal'on militsii* — Special Motorized Militia Battalion
SNR	*Sily nemedlennovo reagirovaniya* — Immediate Reaction Force
SOBR	*Spetsial'nyi otdel bystrovo reagirovaniya* — Special Rapid Reaction Detachment
Spetsnaz	*Spetsial'novo naznacheniya* — Special Designation Troops
SVR	*Sluzhba vneshnoi razvedky* — Foreign Intelligence Service
VDV	*Vozdushno-desantnye voiska* — Airborne Landing Troops
VPK	*Voenno-promyshlennaya komissiya* — Military-Industrial Commission
VV	*Vnutrennye voiska* — Interior Troops

INDEX

Foreign policy, 15-16, 28-29, 87-95;
    see also 'New Imperialism' and 'Near Abroad'
FSB (includes earlier incarnations as Security Ministry and FSK), 25, 29, 41, 63-64, 68, 69, 74, 89, 96-104, 105, 106, 108, 110, 117, 120-1, 154
FSK, see FSB
Fyodorov, Boris, 40

GAI, 118
Gaidar, Yegor, 14-15, 16, 20, 21, 40, 74
General Staff, 30, 92, 124, 125-26, 139
Georgia, 6, 11, 47, 51, 55, 77-78, 80, 82-83, 91, 94, 141, 142
Germany, 55, 61, 62, 66, 106, 150
Golushko, Nikolai, 25, 28, 97, 100
Gorbachev, Mikhail, 1-12, 14, 23, 80, 96, 110, 111, 148;
    and August Coup, 9-11, 27-28;
    reform programme, 2-7, 22, 30;
    'syndrome', 22-23
Gosatomnadzor, 60-61
Grachev, General Pavel, 16, 25-26, 28, 69, 70, 74, 107, 113, 119, 123-26, 128, 131, 132, 135, 138
Gromov, General Boris, 25, 69, 70, 73, 113-4, 124
Ground Forces (Army), 12, 38, 125, 126, 129
GRU, 18, 97, 98, 99, 106-7, 110, 140-41, 154
GUO, 96-97, 98, 99, 104, 120-1, 122, 154
Gusinskii, Vladimir (and the Most Group), 18, 37, 101, 109

Hitler, Adolf, 35,
Hungary, 7, 133, 135, 144

Ilyushin, Viktor, 17, 18,
Ingushetia, 44, 45, 46, 47, 65-66,
Interior Ministry (MVD), 6, 9, 12, 25-26, 27, 28, 29, 96, 99, 100, 111-9, 154
Interior Troops (VV), 12, 26, 27, 66, 68, 69, 70, 72, 92, 111, 113, 114-7, 122, 132, 155
Iran, 61, 88, 89, 90
Iraq, 61, 88
Islam, 73, 81, 84, 149
Italy, 33, 41-42, 53, 62, 66, 75

Japan, 33, 41-42, 43, 49, 53, 62-63, 75, 89, 106, 152

Kaliningrad, 48, 52, 78, 91, 128
Kazakhstan, 11, 31, 49, 57-58, 59, 60, 65, 77-78, 93-94, 150
KGB, 1, 9, 12, 17, 19, 29, 62, 63, 89, 96-97, 98, 99, 100, 102, 104, 106, 108,
109, 110, 116, 119, 154
Khasbulatov, Ruslan, 20-21, 23, 24-25, 28
Kobets, General Konstantin, 24, 25
KOGG, 119
Kokoshin, Andrei, 125
Kolesnikov, General Mikhail, 25, 92, 107, 124, 125-26
Korzhakov, General Alexander, 16, 17-19, 37, 41, 67-68, 101, 102, 104, 109,
110, 120-1;
see also SBP
Kozyrev, Andrei, 16, 17, 29, 32, 87-88
KPRF, 34, 154
Kryuchkov, Vladimir, 9, 11
Kulikov, General Anatoli, 71, 113-14
Kyrgyzstan, 11, 57-58, 59, 77-78, 93-94, 119,

Latvia, 11, 77-78;
see also Baltic States
Lebed, General Alexander, 37-39, 40, 125, 131
Lenin, Vladimir, 111
Liberal Democratic Party, see Zhirinovsky
Lithuania, 11, 51, 60, 77-78;
see also Baltic States
Lobov, Oleg, 17
Luzhkov, Yuri, 19, 33, 37

Mari-El, 45, 46, 47
MB, see FSB
MBVB, 100
MEK, 80
Military Doctrine, 29, 30-31, 73, 81-82, 126, 133
MOB, 119
Mobile Forces (MS), 126, 128, 135, 138-40, 143, 154
Moldova, 11, 38-39, 49, 77-78, 83-84, 90, 91, 141-43
Moscow, 14, 17, 19, 24-27, 33, 37, 48, 62, 116, 118, 119-20, 120-1, 149, 151
MUR, 118

Nationalism, 7-8, 16, 20, 21, 33, 38-39, 63, 131-32, 148-49, 150
NATO, 31, 88, 90, 92, 107, 132, 137

Naval Infantry (marines), 70, 134, 137-38, 139, 140, 154
Navy, 60, 78, 129, 132
'Near Abroad', 30-31, 35-36, 40, 46, 76-86, 89, 106, 106-7, 119, 126, 131, 138, 141-43, 146, 148
'New Abroad', 46, 51, 85
'New Imperialism', 35-36, 81-86
Nikolayev, General Andrei, 119, 124-25
Nuclear industry and stockpiles, 3, 17, 58-61, 88, 89, 90, 129

ODON, 114-7, 154
Oil, 66, 105-6, 145
OMON, 12, 27, 118, 122, 154
OMSN, 118
Opnaz, 114, 117
Organized crime, 43, 52-61, 62, 66-67, 75, 76, 107, 109, 113, 117, 118, 151
Ossetia, North and South, 45, 46, 47, 83, 141-43

Parliament, see Supreme Soviet (until 1993) and Duma (after 1993)
Partnership for Peace, 90-92
Patrol-Guard Service (PPS), 27
Pavlov, Valentin, 9-11
Peacekeeping, 38, 80, 82-85, 126, 134, 141-43
Pinochet, Augusto, 6, 22, 37, 39
Poland, 35-36, 52, 76, 90, 150
Police, 12, 24-27, 28, 56, 66, 117-9, 121, 122, 131, 154-55;
    see also Interior Ministry and OMON
Primakov, Yevgeni, 104, 105-6
Pugo, Boris, 9-10, 11

Rapid Reaction Group (GNR), 27
Roman Empire, 147
Russian Federation, rise of, 7-8;
    regions and, 33, 43-51, 53, 128, 147, 149, 150, 151-52
Russian expatriates, 52, 78, 81, 83, 84, 126
Rutskoi, Alexander, 11, 20-21, 23, 24, 25, 28, 34, 39, 121, 124
Rybkin, Ivan, 32

Sakha, 45, 46, 48
Savostyanov, Yevgeni, 74, 102, 120
SBP, 18-19, 37, 97, 98, 99, 101-2, 104, 107, 110, 120-1, 122, 155;
    see also Korzhakov

SBR, 140
Second World War, 1, 2, 34, 85, 119, 135, 137
Security Council, 40, 70, 101, 105, 109, 125
Security Ministry, see FSB
Shakhrai, Sergei, 17, 40
Shevardnadze, Eduard, 6, 10, 83, 87, 91
Siberia, 43, 48, 65, 146, 150, 152
Skokov, Yuri, 33, 34, 39, 40
SKVO, 69
SNR, 138
Sobchak, Anatoli, 33
SOBR, 118
South Korea, 6, 37, 43, 49, 144
Spetsnaz, 27, 55, 106, 134, 138, 139, 140-41, 155
St Petersburg (Leningrad), 12, 33, 48, 58, 59, 62, 118, 149, 151
Stepashin, Sergei, 68, 69, 100, 102, 106, 110
Stalin, Joseph, 1, 2, 8-9, 44, 65, 100, 111, 130
Strategic forces, 60, 123, 126, 128-29
Supreme Soviet, 5, 19-22, 24-8, 29, 30
'Sverdlovsk mafia', 16-17, 19, 33
SVR, 96-97, 98, 99, 101, 102, 104-6, 107, 155

Tajikistan, 11, 25, 58, 59, 60, 63, 77-78, 80, 84, 94, 119, 142-43
Tatarstan, 43, 45, 46, 47, 150, 151
Tax Police (NP), 89, 97, 99, 106, 108-9, 154
Terrorism, 52, 53, 58, 60-1, 62-64, 68, 74, 109
Turkey, 73, 84
Turkmenistan, 11, 63, 77-78, 93, 119
Tyva (Tuva), 43, 45, 46, 47

Udmurtia, 45, 46, 47
Ukraine, 11, 49, 60, 63, 77-78, 81, 84, 90, 91-92, 97, 118, 135, 137-38, 141, 148, 149, 150
United Kingdom (UK), 57, 66, 67, 90, 108, 118, 150
United Nations (UN), 86, 91, 142-43, 152
USA, 1, 41, 42, 52, 61, 62, 66, 75, 90, 105, 108, 118, 123, 137, 150, 152
Uzbekistan, 11, 58, 59, 60, 77-78, 93

VDV, 135
Volkogonov, General Dmitri, 26
VPK, 9

World Bank, 19

Yanaev, Gennadi, 9-10
Yavlinsky, Grigori, 40
Yazov, Dmitri, 9, 126
Yegorov, Nikolai, 68, 69, 70
Yeltsin, Boris, 7, 9-10, 11, 13-23, 24-9, 30, 34, 40-42, 55, 65, 67, 69, 71, 74,
    88, 99-100, 102, 104, 109-10, 120, 121, 123, 124, 125, 131, 145-46, 148;
    and the 1996 elections, 18-19, 34, 40-42, 121, 145-46;
    career, 13-14, 148;
    ideas, 14-15, 16, 22-23, 87, 94, 104
Yerin, Viktor, 28, 68, 111, 113
Yugoslavia, 28, 49, 52, 82, 86, 88, 91, 142-43

Zhirinovsky, Vladimir, 16, 23, 28, 35-36, 40, 76, 85, 91, 93-94, 110, 114,
131-32
Zyuganov, Gennadi, 34